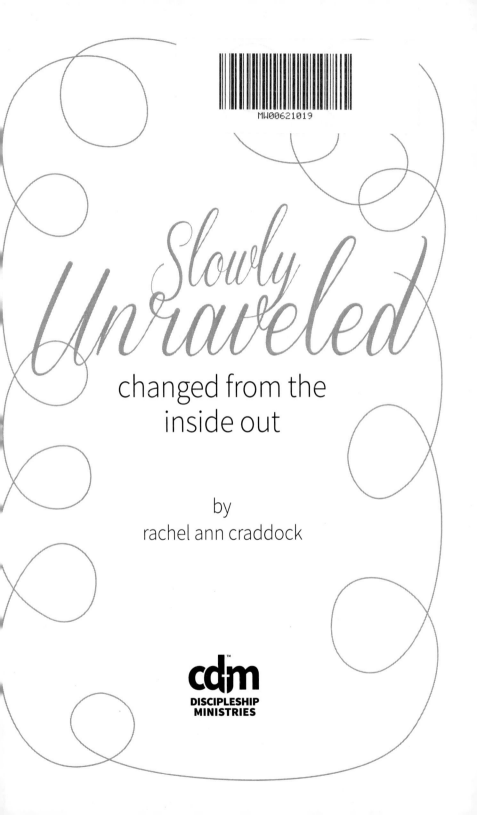

Slowly Unraveled

changed from the inside out

by
rachel ann craddock

cdm™
DISCIPLESHIP
MINISTRIES

MW00621019

**DISCIPLESHIP
MINISTRIES**

©2019 Rachel Ann Craddock

Published by:
Committee on Discipleship Ministries
1700 North Brown Road, Suite 102
Lawrenceville, Georgia 30043

PCA Bookstore: 1-800-283-1357
678-825-1100
www.pcacdm.org/bookstore

Unless otherwise indicated, all quotations from Scripture are from the
English Standard Version of the Bible, copyright 2001 by Crossway Bibles,
a division of Good News Publishers,

All rights reserved. No part of this book may be reproduced, stored
in a retrieval system, or transmitted in any form or by any means—
electronic, mechanical, photocopy, recording, or otherwise—except as
expressly allowed herein or for brief quotations for the purpose of
review or comment without prior permission of the publisher,
Committee on Discipleship Ministries, 1700 North Brown Road,
Suite 102, Lawrenceville, GA 30043.

ISBN: 978-1-944964-37-5

table of contents

Part Five: Parenting

Part Six: Grief

Part Seven: A Redemptive Tapestry

preface

Yes. Outwardly we are wasting away but inwardly
we are being renewed day by day.

2 CORINTHIANS 4:16 (NIV)

*e*veryone has a story. We are all living products of the moments we have experienced in our past; how we interacted with these moments mentally, emotionally, and spiritually, shape the way we live in the present day. In order to better understand how we see ourselves, how we interact with others, and how we interact with God in the present, it is necessary to understand our personal stories and the significant, life-shaping events of our pasts. The understanding of the highs and lows in your personal story will give you a better understanding of yourself, and listening to the highs and lows in the personal stories of others will increase your compassion, empathy, and connectivity to those around you.

> Stories tell me not only who I am but also who you are and what we are together. In fact, without you and your story I cannot know myself and my story. No one's story exists alone. Each is tangled up in countless others. Pull a thread in my story and feel the tremor half a world and two millennia away.
> — **Daniel Taylor**, *Tell Me a Story*[1]

1   Daniel Taylor, *Tell Me a Story* (St. Paul, MN: Bog Walk Press, 2001), 6.

I have written a book about my personal story because for far too long I failed to try to understand and see the beauty in the redemptive story God has been writing for me. My past was something I desired to forget about instead of something I treasured and recognized as an important part of the woman I am becoming. My mother passed away from breast cancer when I was only fourteen years old. After her passing, I struggled with feelings of shame, unworthiness, and not belonging. My family without a mother made me feel like an outsider. For years I tried to find wholeness and I tried to remedy my outsider feelings, but I struggled to find lasting satisfaction in earthly remedies. There was a deeply woven pain I was unable to detach from my inner self.

When I was twenty-one, I understood for the very first time what it means to trust in Jesus and His Work on the cross. A new life given to me in Christ gave me freedom from my old self. I knew I was seen and forgiven by God; however, I still had these threads of shame, unworthiness, and longing to belong woven deeply in the story of my past. As a new Christian, I tried to ignore these deeply woven threads by just covering them up with Scripture, but no matter how hard I tried to forget about the hurtful seasons in my past, the shame and unworthiness always loomed in the shadows.

In the last few years, I have worked hard to look back into the shadows of my past and use God's Word to shine a light on the deeply woven threads of shame, unworthiness, and my longing to belong. Once I brought these little demons into the light, I didn't see my pain in a neat little box; what I saw was many woven layers of pain. When we overcome one layer of shame, unworthiness, and longing to belong, there is always another layer underneath. As I've worked through my personal story over the years, I have seen that I have many lies tangled up with truth in my heart, and because I ignored this shame and these lies for so long, lies and truth became interwoven, making it difficult for me to discern what was a lie and what was truth.

I have had to take a long, hard look at the experiences of my past and unravel the interwoven lies from the truth. This book is a culmination of the work I have done on unraveling my personal story. Just like a sweater unravels, the first thread is the beginning of the unraveling of all the rest. Once you tug on one loose thread, you will soon be left with a hole in the fabric, a hole revealing and exposing what lies underneath the surface. The exposure, or the unraveling, is outside of human comfort and control. It's scary and makes you vulnerable, but the unraveling is necessary and good.

Unraveling is a life-long journey and a daily dance in the gospel where moment by moment we are called to die to ourselves and live for Jesus.

In my experience, my journey in life has been a slow unraveling and pulling apart of the old so I can fully embrace the new. Unraveling is a life-long journey and a daily dance in the gospel where moment by moment we are called to die to ourselves and live for Jesus. I have had to untangle the past from the woman God is making me to be in Christ. In seasons, it has been painful to unravel; I have felt naked, but at the same time, the unraveling has been wonderful and freeing. I am freed as old patterns wisp away, and in the unraveling, I find new life which I have access to only in Christ.

I am not the one doing the work of the unraveling. This transforming change has had to be supernatural. It is God who sees me revealed and exposed, doing the work to carefully unravel. God is completely in control. Jesus, God's Son, is the image of the invisible God. In the New Testament book of Colossians, Jesus is described as the continual sustainer of creation. "He is before all things and in Him all things hold together" (Col. 1:17). Jesus holds all things together to keep them from falling into chaos or unraveling out of control. My patchwork is bound together by Christ in me, the hope of glory. The same power that raised Christ from the dead lives in me through the Holy Spirit. The Holy Spirit has great power over sin, death and the unhealthy threads of shame in my personal story. Little by little, The Greatest Story-Weaver of all is unraveling every measure of my old self. God is taking away my old threads and reweaving new threads bound to Christ by His Spirit.

Being unraveled is not easy, but it is good. Being unraveled little-by-little in the hands of a completely in-control and good God reveals less of me and more of Him. This is the journey I have been traveling. I am a woman, a teacher, a mother, a pastor's wife, and I have been unraveling my personal story and learning how to apply God's Word to fight my feelings of shame, unworthiness, and longing to belong in a moment-by-moment, daily dance of dying to the old self and living for Christ. My hope is that as you read this book, you will think about your own personal story and unravel alongside me on the way. In the unraveling we will see the God who, little-by-little, makes all things new.

He must increase, but I must decrease.

JOHN 3:30

part one

strength

chapter one

old strength

brennan Manning writes, "To live by grace means to acknowl-
edge my whole life story, the light side and the dark side." [1]
So in order to embrace grace, I will begin at what feels like the
dark side. While the threads of my whole life story begin at birth
just like everyone else's, the threads of the dark side of this story
do not begin at the very beginning at all. This story begins several
years later with a girl in the front passenger seat of a silver Chrysler
Town and Country minivan and my father behind the steering
wheel. This is the moment where I see the beginning of my misunderstanding of what it means to be strong in this world.

Threads of Unhealthy Patterns

The March day was gray as our family minivan pulled out of the
driveway. The shift of a new season drew near, but the grayness
of winter still hung over our small town in the Midwest. Tiny
specks of rain made transparent polka dots on the windshield as
the minivan accelerated to twenty-five miles per hour. My father
was driving, and I, a freshman in high school, was sitting in the
passenger seat on the less-than-a-minute ride down Sycamore
Creek Drive. I was certain I found myself alone and without my
younger siblings in the car because my father was going to share
difficult news with me that morning. As I buckled up, I anticipated

---

1 Brennan Manning, *The Ragamuffin Gospel* (Sisters, OR: Multnomah Publishers,
2005), 25.

my father telling me that my mother would not wake up from her coma and she would soon pass away.

My mother's sickness and soon-to-come passing was difficult for me as a young teenager, but not surprising. My mother was diagnosed with breast cancer when I was only seven years old. Throughout my childhood she fought against breast cancer: hair loss, chemotherapy, medical trials, radiation and even a remission during my fourth-grade year. In the early 1990s, my mom tried everything to fight against this disease, but cancer returned shortly after her remission, and during my freshman year in high school, the cancer metastasized to her liver and then to her brain. Eventually, she was in a coma.

In the car with my father, I physically prepared myself for the life-changing words I anticipated: my breath was held, and my muscles were tightened. Intentionally, I looked out the window at the graying scenery because I couldn't look in my father's direction. My mother was a brave, tough woman, and being the oldest daughter, I decided I needed to be brave and tough too. I feared even an ounce of human connection in this moment would leave me knee-deep in a puddle of my own tears. I was broken beneath the surface, but outwardly I wanted to appear tough-enough to be numb to the overwhelming pain I felt inwardly.

To protect myself from the feelings within me, I built a faulty foundation upon all the human strength I could muster up. In this moment, I layered invisible walls between my father and me; to flee connection, I gazed out of the window and focused on the blurring line where the curb met the grass. I filled my lungs with every ounce of strength I could find in every square inch of the minivan. While I held my breath, my inner monologue chanted ugliness: "Weakness is not an option, Rachel; you better not cry." In that moment, as a young teenager, I did not give myself permission to grieve. As I focused on the line streaking out of my window, my father spoke the life-changing words: "Rach, you know Mom is going to die."

I can't imagine how difficult it was for him to tell me those eight words. I didn't have to look in my father's direction; his words were filled with grief. Even through the invisible walls I had built between us for the sake of my own self-protection, I felt the weight of the grief in his words tangled up together with the grief and brokenness inside my own heart. The wounds of my mother's sickness and her approaching death quickly turned into lies which whispered, "Without my mother, I am all alone in this world." The lies of walking through grief in isolation turned into vows of self-protection.

Even with my breath held, longing to disengage from the moment, the tears came to my eyes, and the two distinct lines of curb and grass I watched began to swirl together. In all the human strength I could physically muster up, the tears came anyway. The faulty foundation of all my human strength could not hold back the depths of the pain I felt in that moment.

When I caught my reflection in the window, I could see my father's reflection watching mine. Immediately, I was overcome with disappointment in myself. My reflection revealed there were tears in my eyes, and I felt ashamed. I knew if I could see the tears in my reflection in the window, my father could see them too. I felt shame in that moment because I saw my tears as a sign of personal weakness. Reacting out of my woundedness, with a vow of self-protection, I became frustrated with myself for the tears I cried over the approaching death of my mother.

In that shame-filled moment, I began to wire my inner self for more self-protection. Standing on a faulty foundation of human effort, I began to thread unhealthy patterns. My shame led me to believe human strength has no time for anger, sadness, tears, or grief. This wound of my mother's soon-to-come passing was the beginning of the lie I once believed: tears are a sign of personal weakness. Tangled-up in this lie, I vowed to muster up more human strength to be stronger the next time disappointment crossed my path in life.

Pulling Up Bootstraps on a Faulty Foundation

The memory of that moment is longer than the moment itself. Or perhaps, the memory of that moment has been stretched out and hangs onto everything about me. Each thread has been wrung out and revisited so many times like a stretched-out wool sweater left on a metal hanger to dry for much too long. That moment, less than a minute in time, and the memory, the pieces my brain has tucked and filed away, seem to have traveled around the world—through time and back again. The wrung-out and revisited threads stretch and weave into my story across years, seasons, places, and relationships.

Peering back into that moment, I know my mother's passing will always be a deeply woven thread in the story God is writing for me. Unfortunately, at the age of fourteen, with a tangled-up view of strength, I did not permit myself to become sad. Instead, I built what I believed was strength upon the faulty foundation of human effort. I learned to try harder. I learned to be stronger. I learned to bury feelings of inadequacy. I learned to accept what life throws my way with the appearance of a smile.

When sadness is seen as weakness, it is easy to hide and bury what is believed to be negative emotion. On the exterior, I wanted to appear to be tough. My nature was to pull up bootstraps, march on, and hold all things together on my own. This tangled-up desire came from longing to appear strong on a faulty foundation and from a misunderstanding of strength.

Faulty foundations built upon human strength are shallow, as shallow as a thin layer of ice atop a neighborhood pond. When I revisit this memory, this story-defining moment in my personal misunderstanding of strength, I see a fourteen-year-old girl building walls around her heart in the name of self-protection. Underneath the layers of self-protection on the faulty foundation of human effort bubble fear, uncertainty, anger, and sadness.

As I go back to the long, drawn-out threads of that moment, I can't reconcile which I am more upset about: the news of my mother's approaching death, or the shame I felt because I cried about it.

> Shame is life-dominating and stubborn. Once entrenched in your heart and mind, it is a squatter that refuses to leave. — **Edward T. Welch**, *Shame Interrupted: How God Lifts the Pain of Worthlessness and Rejection*[2]

---

[2] Edward T. Welch, *Shame Interrupted: How God Lifts the Pain of Worthlessness and Rejection* (Greensboro, NC: New Growth Press, 2012), 12.

Shame leads people to develop unhealthy patterns. Shame is present in the first chapters of the Bible, right after the creation of a perfect world. God created Adam and Eve in the Garden and everything was very good. Adam and Eve were both naked and unashamed as they walked with and were in community with God. "And the man and the woman were both naked and not ashamed" (Gen. 2:25). Work, marriage, identity, and creation were all very good in the beginning; shame and brokenness did not exist before Genesis chapter 3.

> Now the serpent was more crafty than any other beast of the field that the Lord God had made. He said to the woman, "Did God actually say, 'You shall not eat of any tree in the garden?' And the woman said to the serpent, "We may eat of the fruit of the trees in the garden, but God said, 'You shall not eat of the fruit of the tree that is in the midst of the garden, neither shall you touch it, lest you die.'" But the serpent said to the woman, "You will not surely die. For God knows that when you eat of it your eyes will be opened, and you will be like God, knowing good and evil." So when the woman saw that the tree was good for food, and that it was a delight to the eyes, and that the tree was to be desired to make one wise, she took of its fruit and ate, and she also gave some to her husband who was with her, and he ate. Then the eyes of both were opened, and they knew that they were naked. And they sewed fig leaves together and made themselves loincloths. And they heard the sound of the Lord God walking in the garden in the cool of the day, and the man and his wife hid themselves from the presence of the Lord God among the trees of the garden. But the Lord God called to the man and said to him, "Where are you?" And he said, "I heard the sound of you in the garden, and I was afraid, because I was naked, and I hid myself." — GENESIS 3:1-10

Fear, shame, woundedness, and brokenness enter the world in Genesis 3. Adam and Eve disobeyed God's one command to them, and immediately following, they feel fear and shame. In their nakedness they are no longer unashamed as they were in the very good beginning. After they ate the fruit, they felt exposed and they longed to be hidden. In the present day we still feel the ripple effects of this first transgression. We were created for glory, but because of Adam and Eve's first transgression we now experience fear, shame, woundedness and brokenness in life here on Earth.

What is shame? Sometimes shame is thought of as something similar to guilt, but there is a difference between guilt and shame. Guilt is feeling broken over something you have done, but shame is the feeling of nakedness and the longing to hide. Shame causes us to hide who we really are beneath the appearance of a cleaned-up surface, because shame tangles up the way we see ourselves in the world. Brené Brown is a shame expert; in her book *Daring Greatly* she writes, "I define shame as the intensely painful feeling or experience of believing that we are flawed and therefore unworthy of love and belonging."[3]

In that moment, crying as a fourteen-year-old girl after hearing the news of my mother's soon-to-come passing, I didn't feel guilt over the tears. What I felt was deeper; I felt like there was something wrong with the kind of person I was in that moment. The threads of this shameful feeling were woven in my misunderstanding of strength. The feeling of shame led me to a place where I felt unworthy in this world because of my mother's inevitable passing, the brokenness of our family, and the weight of the grief feelings within me that I longed to hide from the outside world.

The human desire to correct and control takes over when we feel shame. In shame-struggles we find ourselves in hiding. We as humans cannot let anyone see there is something wrong with us. Shame leads us to retreat into isolation. In a world of selfie filters, Botox, and weight loss pills, we have learned to quickly clean up and hide the least desirable parts of ourselves. Shame causes us to operate just at the surface-level of our hearts. Just like Adam and Eve, we too are afraid of being seen and exposed, so we hide. It

---

3   Brené Brown, *Daring Greatly* (New York: Penguin Random House, 2012), 61.

is because of shame and the longing to hide that we experience meaningless points of connection with others; we are afraid to let others see us in our imperfections, and this is a lonely and isolating way to live.

Standing in a shame-space, I learned tough-girl behaviors and the appearance of strength. The appearance of strength led me to years of hiding behind a false tough-girl exterior. In this tangled-up belief, I found that the more I hid, the less others could see the real me. I believed the more I learned the pattern of hiding, others wouldn't even see the reflection of me, a sad girl with hot tears in her eyes and a broken heart. In my hiding, I discovered a life of bootstrap-pulling-up and thread-winding around the faulty foundation of human effort. The tightness of the threads I wound held my broken heart together. I thought the bootstraps I pulled up high would protect my feet on the journey as I trekked on a false and faulty foundation.

Thankfully, this was only the beginning of the journey. The beginning was the weaving of unhealthy patterns woven in wounds, lies, and vows, and the rest has been the unraveling of each and every unhealthy thread in the story of redemption God is writing for me. Over time, the threads I began weaving around my heart as a young girl and my understanding of strength, as well as the understanding of everything I thought I knew, have been turned inside out and upside down by the gospel.

"Fear not, for I have redeemed you; I have
called you by name, you are mine."

ISAIAH 43:1

chapter two

the tension of old and new strength patterns

So, first things first. Turn to Jesus,
the one who rescues you from shame.

Edward T. Welch, *Shame Interrupted:
How God Lifts the Pain of Worthlessness and Rejection* [1]

Shame is Sticky

Shame is sticky and shame can stick to everything about who we are and how we operate. Throughout my years in high school after my mother's passing, I struggled behind the appearance of a tough girl. Self-protection and the need to hide behind the tough-girl mask were coping mechanisms I used to hide the pain and shame I felt. In my tangled-up view of strength, I had a tangled-up belief that it was wrong for me to be sad. I tried harder to be happy, but in my own human strength, I never felt the wholeness I longed for. I didn't know who I was anymore. I became what others needed me to be. I desperately wanted to fit somewhere after my mother's passing.

I felt shame in many ways as a teenager, shame that I wasn't right. With my mother passing away, my family didn't feel right anymore; therefore, I felt like there was something wrong with

---

1   Welch, *Shame Interrupted: How God Lifts the Pain of Worthlessness and Rejection,* 210.

me. Shame came over the fact that in a perfect little town, my family seemed different than the others; shame made me feel like a square peg in a round-hole type of place. I ended up quitting the dance team I had loved for years because I no longer had a mother to sew my costumes or help me with my makeup like everyone else. Shame is tricky, and shame leads you to believe that because you are different, you are wrong, or even bad. Shame can drag you away from the things you once loved—and shame can cause you to indulge in unhealthy behaviors. If you feel wrong, in shame you believe you might as well do wrong. It is a constant feeling of contamination or dirtiness. I could not shake my shame off me—the shame was stuck to me—shame became the way I saw myself, as if I never fit.

As a high school student, I believed that I no longer fit anywhere, that I was wrong, bad, and contaminated. This led me through seasons where I felt like I was never enough and like I would never fit in. No matter how hard I tried to hide my pain, I couldn't get rid of it. So instead, I numbed myself with other things. By the age of fifteen I was a pack-a-day cigarette smoker, drank alcohol often, used drugs occasionally, went through seasons of cutting, and would be promiscuous with upper classmen at the frequent house parties in our town. The names people called me in this season of rebellion stuck onto the deeply woven threads of my shame.

Shame is sticky, but shame also isolates. When people feel like they don't fit or they are wrong, they hide. They retreat into a shame-space because inviting others into what feels like darkness and chaos is terrifying. It is the feeling of nakedness, fear of being seen and known, and fear that you will always be just not quite enough in this world.

Human strength, rebellion, and a tough-girl attitude were the parts of myself I showed to the world for seven years after my mom passed away. Walls of self-protection kept me safely in my shame-space. I hid my sadness, brokenness, and weakness behind the faulty foundation of human effort, and I wove threads of my tangled-up view around everything, holding it together in my own strength.

I would say I am not the only one who has walked on the path of shame. Anyone who feels like a square peg in a round-hole type of place can experience shame. Any person who comes from a family that feels broken can feel the same feelings I felt after the death of my mother. Separation, death, divorce, infidelity, criminal charges, family secrets—anything that makes your family feel broken can lead you down the path of shame and hiding.

God's Pursuit in the Shame-Spaces

After seven years of hiding behind the faulty foundation of human effort, when I was twenty-one, I heard and understood the gospel for the first time. The gospel is the truth that threads this whole story together, the truth that threads the redemption of the whole world together. Before the foundation of the world, God was writing a story of redemption for me. In my first twenty-one years, I did nothing to earn this redemption, I don't do anything now to earn His favor, and I will not do anything in the future to earn the love of God. It is only because of God's love, grace, and mercy that He pursued me. God pursued me when I wasn't even searching for Him; He pursued me even when I was hiding in my shame-spaces.

I grew up in a religious family, but it wasn't until I was twenty-one that my faith became my own. While hiding in my shame-spaces, I could not grasp the idea of a Heavenly Father and His love for a broken person. On the outside, I looked like an okay person. By the time I reached college, I was over the rebellion stage and tried to numb my pain with good works. I had a steady boyfriend, I attended church, I was in a good sorority, I took twenty-one hours a semester and earned 4.0 report cards. Tough-girl became good-girl during my years in college; I became very task-oriented to distract me from my pain. On paper, I had a good resumé, laden with philanthropic work, good grades, chair of all the committees, but my inner self was a tangled-up mess I hid from the rest of the world. The real me beneath the layers of self-protection was broken, insecure, and uncertain. In college, I believed if I could just clean up the exterior parts of myself, maybe the wrongness and dirtiness I felt within would just disappear. No matter how I tried to heal my woundedness with my own human effort, nothing seemed to work. The rebellion had been only a temporary escape from my pain, and the good works were just the same. Both my tough-girl exterior and the philanthropic sorority girl were outward covers to hide what was going on beneath the surface. The feeling of wholeness I longed for could never be found while I was focused on my outward behaviors. What I needed was a supernatural transformation from the inside out; what I needed was the truth found in the Bible that God pursues people even when they are hiding in shame-spaces, and He unravels them from the deeply woven shame-spaces of their pasts.

The gospel is the truth that threads this whole story together, the truth that threads the redemption of the whole world together.

Just at the right time, as a senior in college, God used the ministry of Campus Outreach and the words from Ephesians 2:8-9 to bring spiritual transformation in my life. *For it is by grace you have been saved, through faith; this is not of your doing, it is a gift of God, you are not saved by what you do* (paraphrased). Even in my occasional church attending in my first twenty-one years, I never felt like I was good enough for church. Shame gave me a constant feeling of unworthiness, and "not enoughness." Deep down there was a woundedness from my past, a woundedness that kept me—even inside the walls of a church service—in shame-space.

The words from Ephesians 2:8-9 began to free me from this shame. It was freeing to hear the truth of the gospel, that we are not saved by what we do. We are saved by Jesus and His death on the cross. *If you confess with your mouth that Jesus is Lord and believe in your heart that God raised him from the dead, you will be saved. For with the heart one believes and is justified, and with the mouth one confesses and is saved* (Rom. 10:9-10). When we believe with all our heart and confess with our mouth that Jesus is Lord, we are made right with God and freed from our shame. Jesus died for our shame. He bore our shame on the cross, and in Him we are freed from the longing to hide.

Coming from a square-peg family without a mother, seasons of rebellion, feeling sad and hiding in a shame-space, and all my good deeds in college to correct for all my bad deeds—none of it mattered. I wasn't saved based upon my human effort. I was only saved when I rested in Christ's death on the cross. There was no spiritual bank account. God pursued me simply because He was writing a redemption story for my life. This feeling of being fully seen by God and still loved by Him was the first time I felt like I could really be seen and known by others. Throughout the book of Ephesians, Paul writes to the church in Ephesus about the truth and freedom of the gospel. In Ephesians, we can see the redemption story God is writing from before the beginning of time (eternity past) to eternal life for those who believe in the new heavens and the new earth (eternity future).

> Blessed be the God and Father of our Lord Jesus Christ, who has blessed us in Christ with every spiritual blessing in the heavenly places, even as he chose us in him before the foundation of the world, that we should be holy and blameless before him. In love he predestined us for adoption to himself as sons through Jesus Christ, according to the purpose of his will, to the praise of his glorious grace, with which he has blessed us in the Beloved. In him we have redemption through his blood, the forgiveness of our trespasses, according to the riches of his grace, which he lavished upon us, in all wisdom and insight making known to us the mystery of his will, according to his purpose, which he set forth in Christ as a plan for the

fullness of time, to unite all things in him, things in
heaven and things on earth. — EPHESIANS 1: 3-10

From eternity past to eternity future, God is redeeming the
whole world. God was writing a redemption story for me. Even
when I tried to hide, God pursued me. Believers are blessed with
every spiritual blessing and were chosen before the foundation
of the world. It is only by His grace we have the redemption and
forgiveness. God's grace is not just dabbed onto us like one would
dab a tiny bit of lip balm onto a lower lip. This grace, this redemption, this forgiveness, and these spiritual blessings are lavished
upon us. The word *lavished* in Greek means to go over and above,
to abound, or to pour over.

Have you ever been a child at the beach next to your sun-safe
mother? Have you felt the sunscreen lavished upon you? Lavished
to the point that your pores can't consume any more UVA protection, so the sunscreen is oozing out of your pores? The lavishing
is over and above what you need, the sunscreen abounds, and you
now reflect the radiance of white UVA protection. This illustration is merely a glimpse of how God lavishes His grace upon all
believers. When God's grace is lavished upon us, the love of God
will ooze out of the pores of believers. That lavishing of grace
reflects His radiance to the whole world. The spiritual blessings,
the redemption of every life from eternity past to eternity future,
the forgiveness in Jesus are all part of the bigger picture to unite
all things to Him, to weave all believers together in Christ.

*In the present day, God pursues us and covers
our shame with the righteousness of Christ.*

God pursues people even when they aren't looking for Him. God did not leave Adam and Eve naked and ashamed. God pursued Adam and Eve while they were hiding; He made clothes for them and He covered them. In the present day, God pursues men and women even in shame-spaces. God pursues those who feel ashamed and unworthy. He pulls them out from hiding, brushes them off, lavishes His love and grace upon them thicker than sunscreen and begins to slowly unravel the unhealthy patterns once wound up in places of pain. In the present day, God pursues us and covers our shame with the righteousness of Christ.

The freedom and the truth of God's Word electrified me as a new Christian. I felt freedom from the shame-spaces, from my past, and freedom from trying so hard to live as a performance-based sorority girl in college. For the first time, I felt free and whole. I couldn't stop reading my Bible, memorizing scripture, and telling others about the freedom of the gospel.

> How quickly we forget what is ours when we become followers of Jesus.
> — **John Stott**, *Ephesians: Building a Community in Christ*[2]

Shame Overshadows Truth

It wasn't long before I forgot the electrifying truth of the gospel: the beautiful, freeing truth that I don't have to be enough—God lavishes His enough-ness upon me. I forgot that I am not saved by what I do, but because of *Who* God is. Eighteen months after understanding the truth from Ephesians with spiritual ears, I found myself on a journey to St. Louis with my husband of six days.

I had met my husband Michael less than a year before we were married. We both were passionate about God's work in our lives and seeing God work in the lives of others. I dreamed of campus ministry. On the flipside, my husband dreamed of being trained to be a pastor in the local church. When my husband proposed to me, he said something like, "If you say yes to marrying me, you are saying

---

2   John Stott, *Ephesians: Building a Community in Christ* (Downers Grove, IL: Inter-Varsity Press, 1998), 9.

yes to a life of serving alongside me in the local church."

As we drove to seminary, I felt a great tension between who I was and who God was making me to be in the gospel. Understanding the gospel with spiritual ears for the first time was the first layer of unraveling in my redemption story, but there were so many other layers beneath the surface I had suppressed with my hiding for so many years. There were so many old patterns woven in my heart, layers and layers of them from years of living behind a large fortress of human strength. As Michael and I moved our lives to St. Louis, for the first time I felt the tension between my old patterns and the truths I had learned in the Bible. I didn't know how to be a pastor's wife, just like I did not know how to be when I lost my mother as a teenager. I found myself on the edge of uncertainty, and my feelings of shame and "not-enoughness" resurfaced easily. As a new Christian in this season of uncertainty, I reverted back to the only behaviors I knew: hiding my shame and feelings of uncertainty behind a performance-based exterior. I thought I could believe the verses I remembered just a little harder and obey a little bit better. Once again, I found myself on the faulty foundation of human effort; however, this time I cognitively knew many verses from the Bible.

The truths I had memorized in the Bible in the last eighteen months were now tangled up together with my misunderstanding of strength. As a brand-new Christian, I took the words from the Bible (from 2 Timothy 2:3—*share in suffering as a good solider of Christ Jesus*) and wove them into my own patchwork of pulling up bootstraps, burying negative uncertainty deep, and pressing down my feelings. For as long as I could remember, I had only known how to operate from a place of self-protection to hide my feelings of shame and unworthiness. When shame took over, I failed to live out what Bob Flayhart from Oak Mountain Presbyterian Church calls a circular gospel-centered waltz: put off the old shame (repentance), be transformed by belief (believe), and obey (live as God calls me to live in His Word). Unraveling does not happen unless there is movement in this circular pattern.

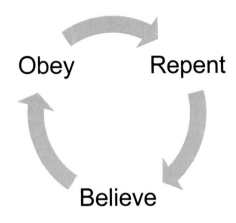

When the words in the Bible are used as a bootstrap-pulling list of rules to obey a little bit better and simply believe a little bit harder, it is legalism, not gospel-centered living. *Legalism* is a term for simply following rules. This is a two-step between obedience and belief. This is not gospel-centered living because it lacks any vulnerability, or the self-awareness needed to repent or put off the old; it omits heart-shedding transformation. When two-stepping between obedience and belief, one may try to believe a scripture just enough with the mind and then try to obey a behavior from scripture without diving down deeply beneath the surface of the heart. This is harmful because both believing hard enough in our minds and obeying well enough with our hands can unintentionally be accomplished in our own human effort. Gospel-centered living requires head, heart, and hands.

I hate legalism but have unintentionally struggled with it in many ways. Dancing back and forth between belief and obedience leaves me tangled up in my unhealthy patterns. I am tangled up and not free. It is frustrating to be tangled up in belief and obedience. On the outside I am trying to believe more, but beneath the surface I am still tangled up in my unhealthy threads of doing everything in my own effort and trying harder. As a new Christian I found myself trying so hard to believe more (belief) and put on the new (obedience) without wanting to dive deep beneath the surface of the unhealthy patterns woven around my heart. I thought believing and obeying were enough, but without the step of repentance, my Gospel Waltz was incomplete.

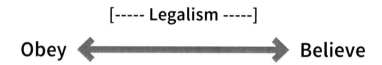

Why is repentance needed? The word *repentance* means to turn away from by walking in the other direction. When new believers understand the gospel and come to Christ for the first time, I believe many come with a desire to repent or to turn away from their old patterns. I desired to turn away from my old patterns as a brand-new Christian, but after my initial life change, I failed to be in a constant habit of being aware of my old patterns and being watchful and intentional to repent of them. I failed to recognize that repentance doesn't happen one time when we first believe in Christ; repentance happens daily. Without self-awareness and repentance, I was disconnected from my heart and tangled up in what I knew and what I could do.

Without repentance legalism turns 2 Timothy 2:3 into something humans can do in their own strength. This is not gospel-centered living. In gospel-centered living we depend on the power of Christ that lives inside of us to change us from the inside out. This happens by the transforming power of the Holy Spirit. The Holy Spirit enters the life of Christians once they depend on His death alone and trust that Christ's death is enough to restore the broken relationship between them and God. The Holy Spirit causes us to be able to hear and see spiritual things around us and to be sensitive and aware of the old patterns we have tangled up in our hearts. As we grow in spiritual living, we should be growing in our dependence, allowing the Holy Spirit to lead us, guide us, and help us to live out the gospel.

> "If you love me, you will keep my commandments. And I will ask the Father, and he will give you another

Helper, to be with you forever, even the Spirit of truth, whom the world cannot receive, because it neither sees him nor knows him. You know him, for he dwells with you and will be in you." — JOHN 14:15-17

Spiritual transformation does not occur without the work of the Holy Spirit, and the Holy Spirit is quenched when we don't dive down into the unredeemed places in our hearts. A stack of memory cards is merely more knowledge woven into the patchwork of learned behaviors. It is only when we put off the old through self-awareness and repentance, rely on the Spirit, and wait on the slow transformation of Christ in us, the hope of glory, that Christians experience true transformation. You cannot be transformed and made new without repentance and the daily unraveling away of the old self.

Mission Exploratory

Despite my outward legalism and my inner struggles of shame and hiding, moving to the Gateway to the West excited me. I had spent the last year of my life as an American history teacher to at-risk fifth graders in Lexington, Kentucky. Most recently, we had studied the Louisiana Purchase and Westward Expansion. The songs I had taught to my students about Lewis, Clark, and Sacajawea still hummed in my head. *Lewis and Clark on a mission exploratory. Boldly searched the great unknown.* The newness of this journey with my new husband filled my heart with excitement; the unknowns about what it meant to be a pastor's wife paralyzed me. I felt like I, too, was embarking upon a mission exploratory to boldly search the great unknown of church leadership.

I barely knew how to attend church at this point in my life as a new Christian. I wondered, how was I going to be an adequate pastor's wife? What even was an adequate pastor's wife? Could I be a pastor's wife with the threads I had woven in seasons of rebellion? In St. Louis, I wrestled with my demons. Even knowing the truth of the gospel of grace, I let my demons consume me. Eventually, I retreated back into my shame-spaces. Only this time

I hid behind a stack of scripture memory cards. I knew the words of the Bible, but I used Scripture as a tool to protect, instead of a balm to transform the heart. When a negative feeling surfaced, I used the Bible to help me correct my behaviors, without waiting on the transforming power of the gospel.

I didn't know how to be truly free of my shame. I only knew how to self-protect behind a false exterior of tough-girl strength and bootstrap-pulling. I didn't know how to be the wife of a seminary student, so I hid instead. When shame is louder than the gospel, it is impossible to experience the freedom of the gospel lavished upon us in Christ.

Just like the heroes and the heroine of Westward Expansion on their mission to boldly search the great unknown, the Christian life is a spiritual journey. The Christian life is not a physical trekking of three thousand miles across the Louisiana Purchase in the 1800s during a long hard winter. This call to live a new life as a spiritual person is an emotional unraveling of old patterns of unhealthy living, the transformation of the inner self, and a command to walk in new spiritual patterns. It is only when we walk the path to boldly search the great unknown that we can learn which foundations are faulty. On this mission as we walk across the unhealthy threads that wind across times, seasons, and relationships, those old bootstraps will eventually wear out, and we will learn to trust the firm foundation of Jesus as the safe place to walk upon with bare and soft soles.

"I have said these things to you, that in me you may
have peace. In the world you will have tribulation.
But take heart; I have overcome the world."

JOHN 16:33

chapter three

the gospel unravels
old strength

I keep asking that the God of our Lord Jesus Christ,
the glorious Father, may give you the Spirit of wisdom
and revelation, so that you may know him better.
I pray that the eyes of your heart may be enlightened
in order that you may know the hope to which
he has called you, the riches of his
glorious inheritance in his holy people, and his
incomparably great power for us who believe.

EPHESIANS 1:17-19a (NIV)

Hiding in Ministry

During the seven years alongside my husband in youth ministry,
I mastered the craft of how to hide behind the mask of a tough
girl. I continued to march on with my bootstraps pulled up high
and a man-centered view of strength. Shame and unworthiness
continued to loom behind me, but I was well-rehearsed at hiding
my feelings of weakness, shame, and unworthiness behind my
theology. Cognitively, I knew the appropriate Sunday School
answers, but the eyes of my heart were not enlightened by the

freedom of the gospel. I still lived as one who was chained by the slavery of performance-based faith instead of one who was truly free in the love of Jesus. I still carried the yoke of slavery to needing to hold everything together in my own human strength.

Parenting made it much easier to hide. When we transitioned from St. Louis to serving at North Cincinnati Community Church, God gave us the stretching gift of three boys in three years. Tending to my children, keeping up with my home, and serving alongside my husband in ministry all kept me busy enough to keep on practicing my legalistic view of *I can do all things through Christ who strengthens me* (Phil. 4:13). Parenting three baby boys in the pew continuously had me under the yoke of slavery of looking strong, performing the task of parenting well, and relying on my own human gifting.

> It is for freedom that Christ has set us free. Stand firm, then, and do not let yourselves be burdened again by a yoke of slavery. — GALATIANS 5:1 (NIV)

Church Planting Assessment Center

One year after our third child was born, Michael and I decided to attend church-planting assessment center to discern the next steps God was calling us to in ministry. Church planting is a term for starting a new church. In our denomination couples attend a three-day training called Church Planting Assessment Center. I would compare church-planting assessment to Hollywood Week on *American Idol*. Church-planting assessment was emotionally challenging, affirming, encouraging, and the chance of someone crying was almost inevitable. I, the tough girl, happened to be the one who cried.

A Faulty Foundation Quakes Easily

I approached going to church-planting assessment as a tough girl, a legalistic version of "I can do all things through Christ who strengthens me," with an emphasis on the "I can do all things." I viewed belief in Jesus as a super power. Belief in Jesus is a supernatural power; it just doesn't work like Wonder Woman's superhuman agility reflexes.

Those being assessed need to select a few men and women to fill out surveys about them to gain data on how the ministry couple interact with those whom they serve. Michael had selected a few men to fill out his forms. One of them commented on Michael's strong Christian background (Michael is a pastor's kid.) and my very limited Christian background. He saw Michael as being able to fly through the process of assessment center, but this man did not feel I would personally be able to attain the approval of the assessors because I had not been a Christian long enough to be able to pass at assessment center as an adequate pastor's wife.

I gathered feedback from women who had been alongside me in ministry. By this point in ministry, I had led many youth group Bible studies as well as discipleship groups. I also participated in our church's women's ministry by attending weekly Bible Study. I performed these tasks well. I kept my house tidy, I showed up, I did my homework, and I cognitively knew the right answers. In my legalism, on paper, my resumé appeared to be perfect. It was the eyes of my heart not yet being enlightened that was the problem. I still had deeply woven threads of shame and feelings of unworthiness; I still had not put off the old self.

During this time of gathering feedback for both Michael and me, two women in my life shared two comments which pulled on the threads of my legalism. One woman mentioned she felt I was a spiritually unhealthy person. The other woman commented, "I don't think you will make it at church-planting assessment." These comments combined with the comment given to my husband about me began to fray my threads of holding everything together behind a false exterior of human strength. When shame is sticky, any comment that can possibly inflict shame and unworthiness does. In his book, *The Prodigal God: Recovering the Heart of the Christian Faith*, Timothy Keller writes, "If we say, 'I believe in Jesus,' but it doesn't affect the way we live, the answer is not that now we need to add hard work to our faith so much as that we haven't truly understood or believed in Jesus at all." [1] In this season, I unintentionally added my hard work and performance to the gospel. I needed to unravel my old view of strength, so I could embrace a biblical view of strength. My old view of strength had me tangled up in slavery to my performance. Only a biblical view of strength could change me from the inside out and free me from my performance-based slavery.

Battling the Old Self

There are two ways I battle my old self right before God is about to unravel old patterns and weave new ones. When God unravels the old self, He first reveals worldly patterns developed in seasons of dealing with emotions in an unhealthy way. Once there is self-awareness of the unhealthy pattern, a spiritual person is free to lay down the old patterns and replace the old patterns with a spiritual pattern. This cannot be accomplished without the deep transforming power of the Holy Spirit. Once a person is a new creation in Christ, that person is completely new in Christ (2 Cor. 5:17), given the Holy Spirit (Eph. 1:13-14), and seen as rightly justified by the blood of Jesus (Rom. 4:25). *Justification* at the throne of grace is a one-time act, a one-time applying of His grace through the atonement of the sacrifice of Christ's death on the cross. We are immediately made right with God when He readies hearts to believe in Him. However, our right standing before God doesn't mean we have gone through the Christian "car wash" called the gospel.

On Earth we are living in the now and the not-yet. In our humanity, we deeply feel the pains of this world because this world is not the way it is supposed to be, but at the same time, we know one day God will make all things new by His grace. Earthly bodies will be resurrected, and those bodies will no longer experience pain or cry tears. In the now and the not-yet, we experience pain, tears and sufferings, and we experience the struggle against sin and brokenness. Christians have the supernatural power of Christ living in them, but in the now and the not-yet, there is tension

---

1   Timothy Keller, *The Prodigal God: Recovering the Heart of the Christian Faith* (New York: Penguin Group, 2009), 124.

between the old self and the hope of being transformed into the likeness of Christ.

In the now and the not-yet, there is a process of becoming more holy, which is named sanctification. *Sanctification* is the work of God's grace, a work that is not a one-time act, but an ongoing, unraveling process. Every single day, men and women who proclaim the name of Jesus in the now and the not-yet are battling the desires of the flesh (old self) and the desires of the Spirit (new self). Men and women who proclaim the name of Jesus are battling their humanity against the Spirit of the Lord inside of them.

> But I say, walk by the Spirit and you will not gratify
> the desires of the flesh. For the desires of the flesh
> are against the desires of the Spirit and the desires of
> the Spirit are against the desires of the flesh, for these
> are opposed to one another, to keep you from doing
> the things you want to do. — GALATIANS 5:16-17

In the now and the not-yet, we will battle the desires of the Spirit against the desires of the old self until we die and find ourselves in the arms of Jesus. Yes, Christians are given the Holy Spirit when we believe, but Christians in the now and the not-yet have so much unraveling to do.

I battle the old self in two ways when God is about to go to work as the Great Surgeon and ever so slowly unravel the disease-ridden threads of my old self and old patterns. I battle my self-righteous flesh and I battle the victimized flesh. My self-righteous flesh is deeply rooted in pride and indulges in others-contempt. Mostly, I deal with my self-righteous flesh when it comes to encountering others in my life: my husband, children, family, and friends. My self-righteous flesh, deeply wound up in pride, will always help me self-justify and point the finger of blame away from myself. In moments when I battle my prideful flesh, I feel puffed up and have an "I'll show them" scowl on my face. My self-righteous flesh is a fierce warrior you don't want to mess with.

I experience the victimized flesh when I indulge in self-contempt. The victimized flesh agrees with the other person wholeheartedly and then dives down into the deep trenches of self-pity. This part of my old self is deeply wound up in my unbelief. In my story, I fail to believe that God is making me new. When I battle the old self of self-pity and unbelief, words seep deeply into the woven patchwork I have around my heart, and like a disease, they find similar threads of moments past when I have succumbed to the belief that I am, in fact, not good enough. The more I listen to and the more I store these victim-like, disease-breeding threads, the more they gather and join together, creating a breeding ground for poisonous and victimized thoughts, leading me to self-pity and disdain. This is shame sticking to the other shame threads I have woven around my heart. This way of living dilutes the power of the gospel and leaves us tangled up and unable to see the power of Christ in us.

The Unraveling of My Unhealthy Patterns of Strength

In a tangled-up way, I led myself to believe the three comments my husband and I received leading up to church-planting assessment were battled in the self-righteous old self. In my story when I find myself feeling like I am not-enough, my natural reaction is to cover this feeling of unworthiness with more performance. I believed I had sewn these undesirable comments to the straps on my boots, and I was ready to march on. I used my knowledge of Scripture memory and my legalism to just put off the comments, try harder, and perform better. What I didn't know was that these comments, said by entirely different people at entirely different times, had actually attached to my victimized, self-pity, disease-breeding threads. These comments pulled on the threads of shame and unworthiness in my story. I had no idea God could be gracious and merciful enough to pull on these exact threads. With His gentle and gracious tug, God was going to unravel everything I had once believed about strength and begin to rescue me from my shame and unworthiness.

When Michael and I arrived in Atlanta for church-planting assessment, we entered the conference room as eager people and we chose front row seats. The room was filled with eighteen of our peers and a long table of nearly as many assessors. In the days that followed we shared about ourselves as a couple, our story, and why we felt a calling to plant a new church. The assessors randomly assigned a time to each couple throughout the week; the assignments were not shared with those being assessed. My desire was to share first. Personally, I could not sit in a conference room chair marinating on the things I had to say. I wanted to get the challenging part of assessment center over with. I wanted to perform well and experience assessment center in a microwave.

In God's good plan and perfect timing, Michael and I did not get the opportunity to stand up in front of the room first; we did not even get the opportunity to share on the first day. Instead, I was called to sit in the front row and wait, forced to marinate in and battle my shame-spaces. While I waited, I had the chance to hear the stories of others and I wrestled with the victim-like threads of not being good enough I had woven around my heart. In the waiting-space, I wrestled with the fact that I, even with all the human strength I could muster up on my own, was not good enough at all. During the long marinating process, I wrestled with every single demon.

Our turn to share from up front came sometime during the second day. Before we stood in the front of the room, a pastor who was one of the assessors, sat next to me during lunch. In our conversation, I was comfortable giving right-response answers and sharing safe, comfortable stories. I was completely fine just operating above the surface of my heart.

Over time, I had developed a way to answer deep questions that came my way about the death of my mother, and because I operated out of self-protection, I had become very clever about what I could say without ever really going too deep. This pastor wouldn't let me just stay in the comfortable shallow waters of my rote and rehearsed responses. In love, he encouraged me out of the shame space, cared for me, and continued to ask questions. He asked me questions until I came to the end of the rote responses I had been rehearsing for fourteen years. Somehow, I found myself at the end of the things I had always said, and at the lunch table I was crying. I was crying right at a cafeteria table surrounded by forty strangers. The mixture of the three comments from my mentors leading up to assessment center, my faulty foundation of human effort, and my life so deeply threaded with shame brought me to a place where I realized all the human effort I could muster up was not enough.

After lunch a pastor preached a sermon from 2 Corinthians 12: *"But he said to me, 'My grace is sufficient for you, for my power is made perfect in weakness.' Therefore, I will boast all the more gladly of my weaknesses, so that the power of Christ may rest upon me. For the sake of Christ, then, I am content with weaknesses, insults, hardships, persecutions, and calamities. For when I am weak, then I am strong"* (2 Cor. 12:9-10).

I have so many expectations that aren't grounded in what God requires of me at all. All God requires is that when I am weak, His power is perfectly displayed.

My personal brokenness, my exhaustion from trying to appear "okay" and "just fine" for so many years and this sermon were the perfect recipe for God to begin to unravel my worldly ideas of what it meant to be strong. Sitting in a conference room, after walking with Christ for seven years, I heard 2 Corinthians 12:9-10 with spiritual ears. In this moment, the words of Scripture were not just knowledge to store in my head, but words that enlightened the eyes of my heart. God's power is made perfect in weakness? God's grace is enough? I can be content and even boast about my weak places because the power of God rests upon me? Weakness is strength?

As I sat there in the conference room, tears still so close to the surface from lunch, I thought about these truths from 2 Corinthians, about the gospel, about a life of pulling up bootstraps and covering up weaknesses. My thoughts shifted back and forth over the years of hiding in a shame-space and feelings of unworthiness. I thought about the years spent as a new Christian covering up weaknesses with Scripture, still trying to perform, using Scripture as a tool to protect instead of a balm to transform. Everything I thought about what it meant to be strong was challenged by God's Word. I knew I was not content in my weaknesses, I knew I tried to hide my hardships. Up until this point, I believed it was socially unacceptable to boast in weaknesses.

Crying at the Podium

Michael and I were invited to share from the podium after this sermon was preached, right as I sat there mentally rewriting all of the things I wanted to say, my tears still close to the surface. All the prepared words written out of a tangled-up view of strength now were unraveled in pieces around me; I tried to pick them up and bring them to the podium.

Michael preached a short sermon and then shared his testimony. When my turn came, my view of human strength and the words I had just heard on spiritual strength collided. As I spoke, some words came out of my mouth that I knew and had rehearsed. Some words I said in front of the crowd I didn't plan on saying at all. I uttered words about feeling a deep burden and need for planting churches to bring the hope of Jesus to others, and then—tears. I began to cry! In front of a room of my peers and a long table of assessors, I broke out into a hot mess of tears. The next words I said went something like, "I want to plant a church, but I have heard that I haven't been a Christian for long enough to be a good church-planting wife. Maybe I won't be good enough because I just don't know all the church songs."

In all my preparedness and pulling up bootstraps, I stood in front of the room and ended up sobbing over not knowing *all* the church songs. My clenched jaw, the gatekeeper of all of those tears, opened wide and every single tear bottled up for fifteen years began to flow. The branch fell and gently touched the surface of my frozen pond. I cracked open completely. For a moment, I was self-aware enough to be broken.

This was the beginning of the gospel unraveling my ideas about strength, my learned behaviors of gate-keeping tears and hiding in shame-spaces and verses. This was when I began to see I have much unraveling to do beneath the surface. I have so many personal requirements for how I believe I should live as a wife, mother and Christian, so many expectations that aren't grounded in what God requires of me at all. All God requires is that when I am weak, His power is perfectly displayed. As I bravely walk in vulnerability, owning brokenness, and rejoicing over healing tears, God is slowly unraveling how I used to define strength, and I am learning to live as God defines strength.

Following Jesus isn't about being good enough, living a moral life or how well we can clean ourselves up on the outside. Cleaning up the outer self is easy. The masks we wear are the easiest things to put off and put on. The gospel is the supernatural power that turns the inner self upside down and inside out. This supernatural power is not like Wonder Woman's superhuman agility reflexes. In contrast, the gospel is the power to save us from our tangled-up desires where we see ourselves as superhuman. Christians aren't being made into cape-wearing superhumans. Christians are being unraveled from man-centered humanity.

Gospel-centered strength is our brokenness and our willingness to let Jesus shine through the broken places. There are many instances where I am still the insecure, guarded girl in the front seat of the Chrysler Town and Country minivan or the legalistic, soon-to-be pastor's wife in hiding. God isn't completely finished with me yet, but He is working to unravel, ever so slowly, my unhealthy patterns threaded in my shame-space.

If we confess with our mouths that we are Christians, I think we need to ask ourselves: Are we tangled up in the head-and-hands faith of legalism, or are we unraveling in the head-*heart*-and-hands freedom of the gospel? Are there holes in your patchwork where others can see the power of Jesus shining through the broken places?

> I am sure of this, that he who began a good work
> in you will bring it to completion at the day of Christ.
>
> PHILIPPIANS 1:6

part two

identity

old identity

And you were dead in the trespasses and sins in which you once walked, following the course of this world, following the prince of the power of the air, the spirit that is now at work in the sons of disobedience—among whom we all once lived in the passions of our flesh, carrying out the desires of the body and the mind, and were by nature children of wrath, like the rest of mankind. But God, being rich in mercy, because of the great love with which he loved us, even when we were dead in our trespasses, made us alive together with Christ—by grace you have been saved—and raised us up with him and seated us with him in the heavenly places in Christ Jesus, so that in the coming ages he might show the immeasurable riches of his grace in kindness toward us in Christ Jesus. For by grace you have been saved through faith. And this is not your own doing; it is the gift of God, not a result of works, so that no one may boast. For we are his workmanship, created in Christ Jesus for good works, which God prepared beforehand, that we should walk in them.

EPHESIANS 2:1-10

Wounds, Lies, and Vows

After the death of my mother, I became deeply wound up in shame. Through my tangled-up desire to appear tough and strong, I became rebellious. During my high school years, I struggled with depression deeply beneath the surface, but covered up my woundedness with addiction. I became addicted to anything that helped detach me from my pain. Cigarettes, alcohol, men, and even drugs all temporarily soothed me and helped me escape my depression. Addiction became the center of my world. This did not make me very popular with the Christian kids in my high school. Many of the nice kids were told by their parents to stay away from me and my bad influences.

In my woundedness, I began to believe lies that, because of my depression, shame, and addiction, Christian families didn't like me. These lies then turned into vows: "I will never be good enough to be a Christian, so therefore, I vow I will never be a Christian." My shame was fertile soil for these wounds, lies, and vows to become deeply woven threads in my story.

When I left my hometown for college, I desired to run as far away from my old self as I could. In college, I believed I could correct my behaviors rooted in rebellion and embrace a new identity. The problem with this was, because of shame, no matter how much I tried to clean up my outward behaviors, inwardly I never felt whole. My wounds, lies, and vows were ever present in every corner of my heart.

Image-Bearers Created for Glory

In the book of Genesis, the Bible teaches that we are all image-bearers of God. God created each of us uniquely in His own image. A person reflects the image of the God who made the most majestic mountains and the rising and falling of the waves on the shore of the sea. We marvel at creation and the created because it was all designed by a very Good Designer. All of creation is made to reflect the glory and majesty of God. This makes it impossible to run from the old self, because even the old self was created to bring glory to God.

God created man in his own image, in the image
of God he created him; male and female he created
them. — GENESIS 1:27

For you formed my inward parts; you knitted me
together in my mother's womb. I praise you, for I am
fearfully and wonderfully made. Wonderful are your
works; my soul knows it very well. — PSALM 139:13-14

Before I really had a personal relationship with the God of the
Bible, part of me was drawn to Him. As an image-bearer, I considered church, I considered moral life, I considered doing good.
I even prayed every single night, "Now I lay me down to sleep, I
pray the Lord my soul to keep, guide me safely through the night
and wake me with the morning light." I had no idea what I was
really praying, but even before I really understood what the Bible
taught about anything, I was drawn to the Creator.

Tangled-Up Image Bearing

At the same time, in the now and the not-yet, the Bible teaches
that the human nature is corrupted because of the Fall. In the
now and the not-yet, humans are image-bearers of God, and at
the same time, the deepest desires of the human heart are in-
fluenced and corrupted by what the Bible calls sin. Sin, just like
shame, is a ripple effect from the first transgression of Adam and
Eve in the Garden.

Before I had read the Bible for myself, I didn't care for the
word sin, nor did I understand it. I knew I wasn't perfect, but
I didn't believe I was bad enough to sin. I knew the basics of
the Ten Commandments, and in my limited understanding, I
believed I upheld most of them. To me, the word sin was for
murderers and prisoners, what I considered the very worst of
people. It wasn't until I really considered the words from Luke
10, when a lawyer asked Jesus what is the most important commandment, and Jesus replied, "You shall love the Lord your God
with all your heart, all your soul, all your strength and all your

mind and you should love your neighbor as yourself" that I was able to consider my own falling short of truth.

Although we are image-bearers, we will not be able to love God with all our hearts, all our souls, all our strength, and all our minds if we try to do this on our own accord. In Genesis 2, God creates everything, and He calls His creation very good. Directly following in Genesis 3, His good creation, man, eats the fruit of the tree, which God has told him not to eat. The Bible teaches that the good promise God made with Adam in Genesis 2:17 is immediately broken in Genesis 3 by the eating of the fruit from the Tree of Knowledge of Good and Evil. The Bible teaches all mankind sinned in Adam and fell with him in this first transgression (1 Cor. 15:21-22).

This is the reason why, no matter how hard the created tries to dwell on the goodness of God, the created cannot love Him with every molecule of their beings. On this side of heaven, we will always fall short of the greatest commandment—all of us will, every moment of every day.

Sin Defined

When I didn't care for the word sin, it was simply because I didn't know the true meaning of the word. I had never understood that sin is a term that simply means to miss the mark. In archery, if you miss the bullseye even by a fraction of a hair, your miss, no matter how close or how far, is called a sin. Think about how many times we miss the mark of loving God with all our hearts, all our minds, all our souls and all our strength. Even missing this by a tiny hair makes you a sinner in need of God's forgiveness and grace.

> We aren't sinners because we sin. We sin because we are sinners.[1] — **R.C. Sproul**

In the book of Romans, Paul writes to the church in Rome about how all have sinned and fallen short of the glory of God (Rom.

---

1   Matt Smethurst, "40 Quotes form R.C. Sproul (1939-1927)," The Gospel Coalition, December 14, 2017, https://www.thegospelcoalition.org/article/40-quotes-rc-sproul/.

3:23). All of us love other things more than we love God. We love our jobs, our spouses, our children, and ourselves. We love our sports teams with all our hearts, all our minds, all our souls, and all our strength when we sit on the edge of the couch, breath held, waiting for that buzzer, and then arms raised up in the air, shouting and screaming after victory belongs to our favorite team. As fallen people, we worship the created much more often than we worship the Creator.

Broken Cisterns

Our hearts are places that are made to love something with all our hearts, all our souls, all our strength and all our minds, but because all have fallen, we love God *and* other things. Jeremiah 2:13 (NIV) says, "My people have forsaken me, the spring of living water and they have dug their own cisterns, broken cisterns that cannot hold water." God is saying through Jeremiah that we image-bearers, a people He created for His own possession and a people He created for good, continually are searching for things other than God to quench our thirst. The Bible is a story that is entirely about this very thing. God created people, and people are continually prone to wander away from life-giving endless supplies of water to drink from water which is stagnant in muddy pots of clay, pots of clay which are broken and cannot even hold enough stagnant, muddy water to satisfy one's thirst!

My Conversion Story

When I was twenty-one and a senior at Eastern Kentucky University, I heard this truth in a coffee shop, and I considered the gospel for myself for the first time. I was created by a good Creator; I was fallen because of Adam's first transgression; I was missing the mark on loving God with all my heart, all my mind, all my soul and all my strength; and I was quenching my God-given thirst by drinking out of muddy, stagnant pots of clay. The reason I continued to be thirsty was because the things I actually loved with all my heart, all my mind, all my soul and all my strength could never

49

quench my thirst.

For the first time it made sense to me why my heart was never fully satisfied. As a college student in that coffee shop, I realized for the first time I lived for myself. My broken cisterns of muddy stagnant water were cisterns of self-protection, self-centeredness, and self-preservation.

The "If I Could Just, Then I Could" Problem

When one lives life drinking from broken cisterns, it is easy to develop a condition I like to call, the "if I could just, then I could" problem. Drinking from broken cisterns never leaves one fully satisfied, so we are constantly needing more. Our achievements never really fulfill, so we live bouncing from one achievement to another. This is the "if I could just, then I could" problem.

Before understanding the gospel, I lived for my resumé, my idea of a marriage relationship, and a nice, moral suburban family living in a home with a white picket fence and possibly a dog. I lived drinking from a cistern of muddy stagnant water, the unsatisfying life of the American Dream. I was so thoughtful of my own self-preservation. If I could just have a good resumé, then I would get a good enough teaching job. If I could just be pretty enough, then I would attract a handsome enough husband. If I could just be moral enough, balancing out church attendance and my scroll of philanthropy work with nights at the bar, then God would be pleased enough with me. My identity was centered around broken cisterns of performance-based living. I always found myself thirsty for more. Tangled up in the "if I could just, then I could" problem, I never found contentment or peace; I only found anxiety, comparison, envy, and a problem where I never saw myself as enough.

In my broken-cistern living, I was very good at preparing to build my own kingdom. I was very good at living a very self-centered life. The kingdom I was building, or dreamed of building, was the kingdom of Rachel. This is why I was thirsty. This is why I lived in a cycle of needing more accolades on my resumé, why I could never be skinny enough, why I needed to be involved in more fundraising opportunities, why I needed to be nicer to other people, because I deeply desired to be well-liked in the kingdom of Rachel. I was so tired. I was so thirsty. Everything I was drinking from could never ever satisfy my thirst.

God Pursues the Unlikely People

I really didn't ask God to change my life. I do not have a moment when I heard or felt God say, "You are mine." I did spend many nights during that semester awake and restless, reading my Bible and desiring to know more about what the Bible said. The more I read the Bible, the more I learned that the Bible is very relevant to all of our lives. Sally Lloyd Jones in her book, *The Jesus Storybook Bible* writes:

> The Bible is most of all a Story. It's an adventure story about a young hero who comes from a far country to win back his lost treasure. It's a love story about a Prince who leaves his palace—his throne— his everything to rescue the ones he loves. It's like the most wonderful of fairy tales that has come true in real life! You see the best thing about this story is—it's true. There are lots of stories in the Bible, but all the stories are telling one Big Story. The story of how God loves his children and comes to rescue them. It takes the whole Bible to tell that story, and at the center of that story there is a baby. Every story in the Bible whispers his name. He is like the missing piece in the puzzle, the piece that makes all the other pieces of the puzzle fit together and suddenly you can see a beautiful picture.[2]

I don't have a moment when I approached the altar or committed to follow Jesus, but what I know is the threads of my story began to unravel as I read God's story that semester. As I read, I learned that before the foundation of the world, God chose me to

2   Sally Lloyd Jones, *The Jesus Storybook Bible* (Grand Rapids, MI: Zonderkidz, 2007), 17.

be a tiny thread in His greater redemption story. I was a tiny piece of His treasure He had come to rescue. A personal God left His palace in heaven and lived on this fallen earth, a place which made Him weep, to die for me, because He loved me and because of Adam's first transgression and my continuing to miss the mark of loving God with all my heart, all my soul, all my mind, and all my strength.

I needed rescuing.

Every piece of my story whispered His name and my need for Him. Even all those nights as a child when I asked Him in my bed, "Now I lay me down to sleep, I pray, to you Jesus, my soul you'll keep," Jesus was the missing piece to the puzzle of my life, and suddenly I saw something much bigger. I went from half-sightedness to whole-sightedness; I could finally see a bigger picture. God, just at the right time for me, because He is rich in mercy, rescued me from my broken cisterns and my Rachel-kingdom building. Even when I was dead in my trespasses and not looking for God, He pursued me because He loved me and not because of anything I did at all, simply because He formed me. He made me. Before the creation of the world, He chose me. He was going to ever so slowly go to work and unravel all the threads I had wound up tightly around my heart, shatter my cisterns of stagnant water, heal my wounds, conquer the lies I believed were truth, and break the vows woven in my woundedness.

> You have made us for yourself O Lord and our hearts are restless until they rest in you.[3]
> — **Augustine of Hippo**, *Confessions*

When it comes to identity, it is impossible to hit the reset button and forget about the places you come from. God created each person and her story uniquely for His glory. God is redeeming His people and transforming the places where they feel shame. God is making all things new. It is so easy to clean up the outward behaviors. I easily gave up the heavy drinking, the cigarettes, and the

---

3   Augustine of Hippo. *Confessions*. Translated by Philip Burton (New York: Alfred A. Knopf, 2001), 5.

external behaviors rooted in rebellion. What is the hard work in the Christian life is the heart-work of unraveling the wounds, lies, and vows that shape a person's story.

God wants to redeem us from the inside out.
He wants to unravel the wounds, lies,
and vows tangled up in our identity.

A Christian must be able to read Ephesians 2:1-9 through the lens of God's entire redemptive story. Yes, we once walked according to the powers of this world, some of us tangled up in wounds, lies, and vows. But God, being rich in mercy, when we were dead and not searching for God at all, made us alive. This is His gift of grace. We are His workmanship, and He is not just redeeming our outward behaviors. God wants to redeem us from the inside out. God wants to unravel the wounds, lies, and vows tangled up in our identity.

If you want Jesus, you must be willing to accept the honor that goes with the relationship. Your royal status—ascribed to you, not achieved—has been unveiled.[4]

Edward T. Welch, *Shame Interrupted: How God Lifts the Pain of Worthlessness and Rejection*

4   Welch, *Shame Interrupted: How God Lifts the Pain of Worthlessness and Rejection*, 224.

chapter five

the tension between new identity and the girl from total darkness

And he came and preached peace to you who were far off and peace to those who were near. For through him we both have access in one Spirit to the Father. So then you are no longer strangers and aliens, but you are fellow citizens with the saints and members of the household of God, built on the foundation of the apostles and prophets, Christ Jesus himself being the cornerstone in whom the whole structure, being joined together, grows into a holy temple in the Lord. In him you also are being built together into a dwelling place for God by the Spirit.

EPHESIANS 2:17-22

before Michael and I left for seminary, I had a friend and mentor say to me, "Rachel, don't you ever forget that you have the Holy Spirit living inside of you." Even though I knew the truth of the gospel cognitively, when Michael and I first set our feet on seminary soil, I still found myself tangled up in the wounds, lies, and vows of my past. The lie that whispered I wasn't enough to be a pastor's wife and the vow that church people will never like me were deeply woven in my identity. With shame tangled up in my new biblical beliefs, I continued to struggle with seeing my past as big and God as small. Shame clouded everything God said was true about my identity. I forgot that I had been far off and was brought near. I forgot I had the Holy Spirit of the Lord living inside me.

God pursues those who are far off from Him, as well as those who are near. In Jesus, both those who are far off from Him and those who have always been near to Him have access to the same Spirit. The most unlikely converts and those who have grown up in covenantal families are brought together in Jesus. Those who were far off and those who were near have now been united together to grow into a Holy Temple for the Lord. Isn't it a beautiful picture to dwell on the truth that the most unlikely converts and the smartest of theologians are being united in Jesus, to bring glory to God?

When we arrived at seminary, I easily forgot the beautiful gospel picture of those far off being united to those who were near because of Jesus. My not-good-enough shame became a scarlet letter I wore around my neck. The words "not good enough" weighed me down everywhere I went.

The vows I made long before I was a Christian about Christians never liking me for who I was turned my extroversion into introversion. Christian people made me uncomfortable because I didn't want to be seen. I hid from other seminary couples as much as I could. Ruled by shame, I had already made up my mind that there was not a place for my authentic self within the body of Christ.

When Fear Is Bigger Than Faith

In our first week at seminary, I was required to go with my husband to an orientation class. A sweet couple sat behind us, and I truly enjoyed connecting with them. They made me feel at ease, and when they offered us an invitation to come over to their house for dinner, I could not refuse. We shared wine, food, espresso, and a talent show from their two adorable children. It was a lovely time and a sweet gift of hospitality. For the first time, I felt God unraveling my false ideas about seminary and God's people. For a moment I felt not-so-different from anyone at all.

In Jesus, both those who are far off from Him and those who have always been near to Him have access to the same Spirit.

Near the end of the evening, we all got around to sharing our testimonies, the stories of how each of us came to know Jesus and how our lives had been changed by the gospel of grace. I listened to all of the other stories, including my husband's. My husband grew up in a parsonage just feet away from the Baptist church where his father pastored. His mother was a pastoral counselor, and his sister had grown to be an ordained minister and a missionary. My husband has known Jesus since he was six years old. He has had highs and lows like everyone, but he rarely remembers a time when he wasn't processing his life through the Word of God and in the community of God's people.

I shared my story last. From what I recall, I led with, "I heard and understood the gospel for the first time a year and a half ago, and God radically changed my life." I wasn't very far into the telling of my story. With my feet very firmly still planted in shame and fear, I was slowly sharing what I thought would be safe and acceptable. I was insecure at every step and every word. I can't remember much of what else I shared, but I remember the woman sitting across from me in that moment said, "Wow, so you are from like… total darkness." I let the words seep in.

I wasn't sure how to respond. *Like from total darkness.* Total darkness. I was the girl from total darkness. And in that moment, tangled up in fear and drenched with words, I felt like the only person in the entire world who was from total darkness. My feet firmly planted into the soil of fear and shame. These words drenched over me and became woven around my identity.

My fear was bigger than my faith.

Faith Over Fear

If my feet had been standing firmly in faith instead of fear, I would have seen this comment as quite biblical. In Colossians, the Apostle Paul writes, "He has delivered us from the domain of darkness and transferred us to the kingdom of his beloved Son in whom we have redemption, the forgiveness of sins" (Col. 1:13-14).

God, just as He delivered the Israelites from their slavery in Egypt, had delivered me from my own slavery to my Rachel-kingdom building in the domain of darkness in 2004; God had delivered me from the total darkness of a life lived apart from Him in slavery to my idols and transferred me to the kingdom of Jesus.

My new friend sitting across the table was not at all trying to harm me with her biblical, true, and amazingly gospel-centered comment. God brings people from total darkness and transfers them by His grace to be sons and daughters in His kingdom. Girls from total darkness, those who were far off, in Christ, are no longer strangers and aliens, but fellow citizens with the saints and members of the household of God.

The Girl from Total Darkness

With my feet standing firmly in fear, I processed the words, "the girl from total darkness," out of shame-based distortion of my identity. I processed these words with a tangled-up understanding of the gospel deeply woven in wounds, lies, and vows that a future pastor's wife could not be from total darkness at all. I held a tangled-up truth where I believed pastors' wives had to be completely holy and perfect, not from total darkness. I processed these five words out of a misunderstanding of the beautiful picture of being a girl from total darkness chosen and plucked out of that darkness just at the right time because of God's great love and mercy.

The words, "the girl from total darkness," when processed through my tangled-up understanding, attached to my threads of fear and shame in that moment. Just like Galatians 5:17 says, "For the desires of the flesh are against the Spirit, and the desires of the Spirit are against the flesh, for these are opposed to each other to keep you from doing the things you want to do." In this moment in my story, I was given the words, gospel-centered words, "girl from total darkness," but instead of responding in the Spirit, I responded in the wounds, lies, and vows of my flesh.

Galatians 5:16, the verse right before, clearly says, ". . . walk by the Spirit, and you will not gratify the desires of the flesh." In this moment instead of clinging to the Spirit, clinging to love, joy, peace, patience, kindness, goodness, faithfulness, gentleness and self-control (Gal. 5:22-23), I chose to attach the eight words, ("Wow, so you are from like...total darkness") to the disease-breeding flesh, the threads of jealousy and envy which Paul goes on to write about in Galatians 5:20, the desires of the flesh which whispered my demons to me, the demons of unbelief which whispered I am not good enough for God to use me in His kingdom.

In the flesh, jealousy and envy easily grow: jealousy of a story that is not mine instead of joy in how God has uniquely knitted me together for His glory—envy and desire for the gifts of someone entirely different instead of peace about who God has uniquely made me to be. Because I had let these words fall on the threads of unbelief, I saw the looming shadow of who I once was as larger than the light of the gospel.

I walked in unbelief and the desires of my flesh for the entire three years we lived in St. Louis at Covenant Theological Seminary. The eight words meant to encourage, when placed upon fear and shame, led me far away from community and back into my shame-spaces. In my isolation, "the girl from total darkness" became my identity. I forgot the beautiful, redemptive hope of the second part of Colossians 1:13-14 that I once was far off, but now, have been transferred to the kingdom of His beloved Son, in whom I have redemption, the forgiveness of sins. In shame and fear, I could not see the beautiful redemptive story God was writing for me.

"The girl from total darkness," wrapped around my threads of unbelief and became a breeding ground for more wounds, lies, and vows. Shame and fear only helped me focus on the first part of Colossians 1:13-14, the unredeemed truth that I was from the domain of darkness. In my unbelief these words became attached to my identity and how I viewed myself within the church: the only person from total darkness.

the gospel unravels old identity

[Those who were far off] are fellow heirs, members of
the same body, and partakers of the promise in Christ Jesus
through the gospel…For this reason I bow my knees before
the Father, from whom every family in heaven and on earth
is named, that according to the riches of his glory
he may grant you to be strengthened with power through
his Spirit in your inner being, so that Christ may dwell in
your hearts through faith—that you, being rooted and
grounded in love, may have strength to comprehend with
all the saints what is the breadth and length and height
and depth, and to know the love of Christ that surpasses
knowledge, that you may be filled with all the fullness of God.

EPHESIANS 3:6, 14-19

The Christian life is most wholly lived out when one practices a circular three-step "Gospel Waltz" (Flayhart). There must be a putting off of the old (repentance), a renewal of the mind (belief), and a putting on of the new (obedience). This three-step waltz is constant, and I have found that once one layer of my wounds, lies, and vows, is unraveled, there is always another layer underneath. However, most of us only do a two-step. When it came to my identity as a new Christian, I two-stepped between putting off the old and putting on the new: repent, obey, repent, obey. I wanted to be freed from my old identity on my timeline instead of waiting on the slow transforming work of the Spirit. I failed to believe God was changing me from the inside out. My two-stepping between repenting and obeying left me tangled up in moralism. I was only scratching at the surface of the wounds, lies, and vows deeply rooted in my identity.

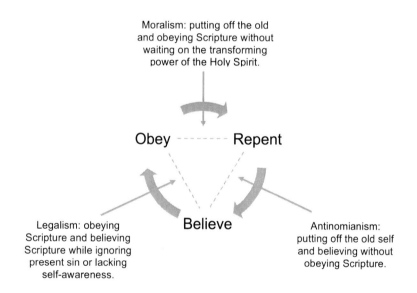

Moralism: putting off the old and obeying Scripture without waiting on the transforming power of the Holy Spirit.

Obey ――――― Repent

Legalism: obeying Scripture and believing Scripture while ignoring present sin or lacking self-awareness.

Believe

Antinomianism: putting off the old self and believing without obeying Scripture.

A Deeper Transformation

In his book, *The Voyage of the Dawn Treader*, C. S. Lewis writes about this idea of surface-level transformation contrasted with heart-level transformation. Eustace Scrubb is a rotten boy and the cousin of the main characters in the Narnia series, Lucy and Edmund Pevensie.

At one point in the story, Eustace has found himself on an island in a cave of treasure. He has placed a bracelet on his wrist and fallen asleep in the cave. When he awakes, he has been transformed into a dragon, an outward manifestation of his inward life. The human-sized bracelet which once was on his boy arm is now on his dragon leg and cutting into his dragon flesh; Eustace is feeling physical pain in this transformation.

Aslan is the Christ-like figure in the Narnia series. He comes to Eustace out of his grace and mercy and tells Eustace he will lead him to a well to bathe his leg. Before Aslan leads him to the well, Eustace will have to undress from his dragon skins. Eustace recognizes the dragon skins are similar to the skins of a snake and reasons he can probably shed his dragon skins in the same way a snake does. Eustace, then in his own effort, begins to scratch the surface of his skin to try to shed his dragon skins on his own. He scratches at the surface, but after several attempts he finds he is unable to shed the deeply painful "knobbly" skins that cover his body.

> I thought to myself, oh dear, however many skins have
> I got to take off? For I was longing to bathe my leg. I
> scratched away for the third time and got off a third
> skin, just like the two others, and stepped out of it.
> But as soon as I looked at myself in the water I knew
> it had been no good.
> — **C. S. Lewis**, *The Voyage of The Dawn Treader* [1]

It is only when Aslan comes to Eustace again and says, "You will have to let me undress you" that Eustace is able to be truly free of his knobbly skins.

> The very first tear he made was so deep that I thought
> it had gone right into my heart. And when he began
> pulling the skin off, it hurt worse than anything I've
> ever felt. The only thing that made me able to bear
> it was just the pleasure of feeling the stuff peel off.

---

1 C.S. Lewis, *The Voyage of The Dawn Treader* (New York: HarperCollins, 2002), 108.

Well, he peeled the beastly stuff right off—just as
I thought I'd done it myself the other three times,
only they hadn't hurt—and there it was lying on the
grass: only ever so much thicker, and darker, and more
knobbly-looking than the others had been . . . I found
that all the pain had gone from my arm. And then I
saw why. I'd turned into a boy again . . . After a bit the
lion took me and dressed me . . . in new clothes.
— **C.S. Lewis**, *The Voyage of the Dawn Treader*[2]

It is interesting to me to think about Eustace and his desire
to change himself quickly, his desire for a quick fix and a quick
healing up of himself. In life on Earth, it is easy to change ourselves at the surface level. Easily we can change the clothes we
wear, the words we use, the beverages we drink, but in the gospel,
God doesn't want us to change merely what is at the surface. God
wants to change us from the inside out. The Christian life has
everything to do with the transformation of what lies beneath
the surface, a transformation which happens when we simply lay
ourselves down and let God do the transforming for us, by His
Spirit. Without waiting on the transforming power of the Spirit,
the Christian life becomes void of the gospel. And when we let
God change us from the inside out, we will find freedom from
the skins that once felt knobbly. God will call you out from the
shame-spaces, and He will dress you in new clothes.

When it came to my identity and "The Girl from Total Darkness," I was unable to live in vulnerable Christian community because I was simply operating at the surface level of my behaviors.
Once again, I found myself trying to quickly polish the surface of
who I was, instead of waiting on God to unravel the wounds, lies,
and vows deeply rooted beneath the surface.

According to the riches of his glory he may grant
you to be strengthened with power through his Spirit
in your inner being, so that Christ may dwell in your
hearts through faith—that you, being rooted and

2   Lewis, 109.

grounded in love, may have strength to comprehend with all the saints what is the breadth and length and height and depth, and to know the love of Christ that surpasses knowledge, that you may be filled with all the fullness of God. — EPHESIANS 3:16-19

In Ephesians 3, Paul writes about this transformation of the inner self. There is power against the old wounds, lies, and vows of our pasts when there is reliance upon the power of spiritual living. Moralism can change a person at a surface level, but Christianity requires inside-out transformation that unravels and redeems the shame-spaces we want to hide beneath the surface. The inner being must be strengthened by the power of the Holy Spirit in order to comprehend the breadth and length and height and depth of God's love for those He draws to Himself. This love surpasses head knowledge; this love fills us with the fullness of God, so we can see our identity as deeply-loved citizens within God's kingdom on earth.

Back to Total Darkness

"If anyone is in Christ, he is a new creation. The old has passed away; behold, the new has come" (2 Cor. 5:17). This was the second verse I memorized as a new Christian in my early twenties. What is funny is, even though I know this verse and am able to recite it from memory, at times, I live as if I don't believe this verse at all.

In 2009, my husband graduated from seminary, and we were called to serve in a church just about twenty miles from my hometown road, Sycamore Creek Drive. God works in mysterious ways: He brought me back to a place I had been running away from for so long. God called me back to a place where I had struggled so I could come face-to-face with my unhealed wounds, lies, and vows.

Knowing 2 Corinthians 5:17 was not enough when we moved back to serve in the suburbs of Ohio. I needed God to transform my inner being with this verse. He did, but this transformation came with the hard work of heart-work. I couldn't just run away from my old self any longer. My old self was a part of me and staring at me right in the face when God called us to serve at North Cincinnati

Community Church. The shame name I wore, "The Girl from Total Darkness," the names I was given during my seasons of rebellion after the death of my mother, and my moving back to a place where I felt like a square peg in a round-hole type of place were the ingredients of a perfect recipe for me to wrestle with my identity in Christ.

I could not two-step away from this central gospel issue. I couldn't merely put off the old self and put on the new self. This type of living left me tangled up in moralism and looking good outwardly, but inwardly I felt so much shame beneath the surface when I was trying to be new all on my own. When I was face-to-face with the person I used to be, I had to gospel waltz around 2 Corinthians 5:17 in a circular motion on a daily basis and unravel the threads of unbelief I had woven when it came to my identity. The transformation only came as I worked to put off the old, waited on the Lord to transform my inner self, and put on the new person God was making me to be. I couldn't just scratch at the surface of my knobbly skins but had to lie down on the grass and let God change me beneath the surface.

> Now this I say and testify in the Lord, that you must
> no longer walk as you used to, due to the hardness
> of heart. You had become callous. But that is not the
> way you learned Christ! Assuming that you have heard
> about him and were taught in him, as the truth is in
> Jesus, to put off your old self, which belongs to your
> former manner of life and to be renewed in the spirit
> of your minds, and to put on the new self, created
> after the likeness of God in true righteousness and
> holiness. — EPHESIANS 4:17-24 (my paraphrase)

John Stott is one of my favorite commentators on Ephesians 4: "There is an emphasis that being, thought and action belong together and must never be separated. For what we are governs how we think and how we think determines how we act. We are God's new society, a people who have put off the old life and put on the new that is what He has made us. So, we need to recall this by the daily renewing of our minds, remembering how we learned the truth in

Jesus and thinking Christianly about ourselves and our new status."[3]

The gospel unravels our identity, our complete identity, not just what we wear, what we say, or what verse we have on our social media accounts. We can change those knobbly skins on our own. We can, like Eustace, in our own strength scratch at the surface of who we are and feel temporary relief, but God does not want us to live a life of surface-deep transformation. God wants to reach in and transform us beneath the surface. God wants every nook and cranny of our hearts to be unraveled from the old and transformed by the new. Christian identity is not something we can do in our own effort. Christian identity comes from the transforming power of Christ in you, the hope of glory (Col. 1:27).

Bloom's Taxonomy

As an educator, Ephesians 4 reminds me of Bloom's Taxonomy of Learning.[4] Bloom's Taxonomy is used in education for designing curriculum. Bloom's shows all of the levels of learning by structuring them into domains. The domains are organized with entry-level learning domains at the bottom of the diagram and complex levels of learning near the top of the diagram.

Remembering is an entry-level cognitive skill, while evaluating is a more complex cognitive skill.

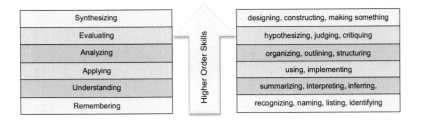

Synthesizing		designing, constructing, making something
Evaluating		hypothesizing, judging, critiquing
Analyzing	Higher Order Skills	organizing, outlining, structuring
Applying		using, implementing
Understanding		summarizing, interpreting, inferring,
Remembering		recognizing, naming, listing, identifying

---

3   John Stott, *Ephesians: Building a Community in Chris.* (Downers Grove, IL: Inter-Varsity Press, 1998), 43.

4   Benjamin Samuel Bloom, *Taxonomy of Educational Objectives, Handbook I: The Cognitive Domain* (New York: David McKay Co Inc., 1956).

When it came to my identity, remembering the words of 2 Corinthians was an entry-level thinking skill, the first step in being taught in the classroom of Christian living. The next level of thinking in Bloom's Taxonomy is understanding, to take the words I had memorized from 2 Corinthians, comprehend what they really meant, and state the truth in my own words. *My old life has passed away and has unraveled from the new. God is making me new, the power of God lives in me and I no longer need to walk in belief that I am still in the domain of darkness. The new has come, I have been transferred to the kingdom of the son He loves* (2 Cor. 5:17 paraphrased).

The third zone of conceptual learning from Bloom's Taxonomy is application, to use this understanding in small concepts of daily life. For example, I returned to my favorite lunch spot in my hometown one day with my children and bumped into a man I had graduated with, and he asked me how I was doing and what I was doing now. When I explained that my husband and I had moved back to Ohio so that he could be an assistant pastor in a Presbyterian church, the man's face became twisted, most likely remembering his previous knowledge of me. He said, "Wow." I could see the unbelief and surprise in his face and I could feel it pulling on my threads of unbelief. Application-level belief in 2 Corinthians 5:17 in this small moment would not lead me to the shadows of my past, condemnation of myself, and feelings of unworthiness, but instead, it led to feelings of praise to the One who has delivered me from the domain of darkness, to the One who has made me new! In the application level of Bloom's Taxonomy, I would apply this Scripture: "The old is gone and the new has come," through the lens of the entire gospel story God is writing for me, and I rejoice at how amazing this truth is for my life and what a beautiful testimony I have.

The fourth zone of Bloom's Taxonomy is analyzing. As a naturally introspective person, I like to analyze information. I like to look back and compare the situations in my life where I walked in belief and unbelief in 2 Corinthians 5:17, to look at my life and see where there is evidence that I am living as one who has been made new. I analyze my new life when I look back and over time remember how, little by little, God is unraveling my unbelief and making me new as I trust in Him, as I believe that I am transferred to the kingdom of the Son with whom He is pleased. The more I let the old unravel and pass away, the more I find myself rooted and grounded on the firm foundation that Christ is transforming me by His grace and by His Spirit. But with analyzing there is wrestling. There are days of unbelief and days of belief. "Sanctification is the work of God's free grace whereby we are renewed in the whole self after the image of God and enabled more and more to die unto sin and live unto righteousness"[5] Little by little the threads of unbelief are unraveled from the patchwork of my heart as I analyze and go back and forth between repentance, belief, and obedience.

Using the fifth zone of Bloom's Taxonomy, I *evaluate* my life through the lens of this truth. I've heard, understood, and can apply 2 Corinthians 5:17 in small, isolated circumstances. I can analyze my heart when I am rooted in this truth, compared to the times I am not rooted in this truth, and now I can live my life through the lens of the old being gone and the new identity having come. The evaluation level of Bloom's Taxonomy of Learning brings me to the place where I can look at those eight words from my seminary days, and after having unraveled all of the untruths about my identity, I can proudly claim the name, "The Girl from Total Darkness." Yes, "I once was lost but now I am found. I was blind but now I see."[6] There is so much beauty in being a "Girl from Total Darkness," so much beauty in the fact that God pursued me, an outsider, and transferred me to the kingdom of His beloved Son.

The sixth and most complex level in Bloom's Taxonomy is synthesizing or creating. This is where a true gospel-centered identity is found. In creating a new pattern of thinking, I can live with a new truth. I am from total darkness, but there is so much beauty in knowing I have been relocated. The old has gone and the new has come. Synthesizing all of life through the words of Scripture and

---

5 *Westminster Shorter Catechism*, Question 35 (Atlanta, GA: PCA Committee on Discipleship Ministry, 1990).

6 John Newton, "Amazing Grace," *Trinity Hymnal* (Atlanta, GA: Great Commission Publications, 1990), 460.

God's redemptive story is so much deeper than just knowing how to recite a verse. Synthesizing helps me see every verse through the lens of God's redemption story. It's to stop running from who I used to be and see that long, looming shadow in the light of the gospel, to forgive myself for the missteps I have made along the way because the God of the universe has forgiven me. Who I was only passes away once it is washed in forgiveness and seen with the eyes of the gospel. I can be moved to thankfulness for a pursuing God who never let go of me even in my seasons of rebellion. I am grateful for all the nights I prayed, "I pray the Lord my soul to keep." He chose me before the foundation of the world.

God wants every nook and cranny of our hearts to be unraveled from the old and transformed by the new.

When it comes to Christian identity, I want everyone to know that believing God is making you new is a process, especially for people who, like me, find themselves wrestling with the real feelings of coming in from the outside and pulling on the unhealthy threads beneath the surface—most especially for rebellious people and "girls from total darkness." If you feel uncomfortable at church, like a square peg in a round-hole-type of place, I want to encourage you to hang in there. Pray that God will penetrate the words from 2 Corinthians 5:17 deeply into your heart and bring you from remembering those words to synthesizing all of your life and situations through God's greater redemptive story. God is the one who calls people to Himself and He knows exactly what He is up to. He transferred you for a reason, so you can be a blessing to the body of Christ.

Maybe you are from total darkness just like I was, and the old has passed away and the new has come. In your new identity you are adopted as a daughter (Gal. 3:26), delighted in, rejoiced over with singing (Zeph. 3:17), fully seen (Gen. 16:13). God is near to you, so near He holds you up with His righteous right hand (Isa. 41:10); you are new (2 Cor. 5:17); God is making you new by His grace and through His Spirit (Phil. 1:6).

It is only when you reach creating a new truth for all of your life, through the lens of the gospel, that you can begin to unravel deeply threaded wounds, lies, and vows from your past. When you can see your entire story through the gospel of grace, you can dismantle vows you made from the lies you believed.

In *The Ragamuffin Gospel*, Brennan Manning writes, *"My deepest awareness of myself is that I am deeply loved by Jesus Christ and I have done nothing to earn it or deserve it."*[7] In my real life I sit in the front row at church almost every Sunday in my orange ballet flats with my four small children in the suburbs just twenty miles down the road from my childhood home. Twenty miles behind me is my past and the girl with her rebellion who kept her distance from a community of believers because of wounds, lies, and vows, but now before me is Jesus, the One who sees me and everything looming behind me in the shadows of my past and cries out, "It is finished, Rachel is mine!"

God plucked me right out of my old life on Sycamore Creek Drive when I wasn't even asking for Him to, dusted me off through unraveling all my unhealthy threads, and changed the course of my steps. Those steps God had planned have led me to where I sit every Sunday: in the front row at church, listening to a sermon from my pastor-husband and raising pastor's kids right among all those good Christian families. I am not worthy, but God has made me worthy, just as He has made all those faces around me worthy. We are all a part of His body, and I trust as I synthesize and evaluate all of my life through my new identity in Him, that God knows exactly what He is up to, even if sometimes I can hardly believe this myself.

---

7   Brennan Manning, *The Ragamuffin Gospel*, 25.

part three

perfectionism

chapter seven

perfectionism, the gospel, and casseroles

I therefore, a prisoner for the Lord, urge you to walk
in a manner worthy of the calling to which you have been
called, with all humility and gentleness, with patience,
bearing with one another in love, eager to maintain
the unity of the Spirit in the bond of peace.
There is one body and one Spirit—just as you were
called to the one hope that belongs to your call—one Lord,
one faith, one baptism, one God and Father of all, who is
over all and through all and in all. But grace was given to each
one of us according to the measure of Christ's gift.

EPHESIANS 4:1-7

I have done many things in seasons of rebellion, but my most
plaguing, ongoing sin is my desire to be perfect all of the time.
At times, I am a slave to perfectionism. I let the unrealistic expectations I have for myself and others tangle up the way I see the
world. This slavery to perfection prohibits me to live in unity in
the body of Christ. This all comes from my misunderstanding of
strength, the need to hold everything together all of the time, and

insecurity about my identity in Christ.

When the desire for perfectionism is greater than my desire to embrace the grace given to me by Christ, I fail to see myself and others around me with the eyes of the gospel. Perfectionism leads me back to a life of living behind a mask; I am disconnected from unity with others because perfection stifles vulnerability.

The Perfect Casserole

Alongside my husband in seminary, in our first few weeks of marriage, he was enrolled in summer classes at Covenant Theological Seminary, and my job as a first-grade teacher didn't begin for a few more weeks. Michael was swamped with alphas and omegas while he studied for Summer Greek. (Greek is a requirement in seminary, so pastors are able to read the New Testament in its original language.) Instead of spending another day at the apartment complex pool alone with a book (I had read seven or eight just in our first month.) or another night over a TV tray in front of *Wheel of Fortune*, I decided I would prepare the house and a meal, so Michael and I could have some new friends over for dinner.

While my husband studied Greek, I tried to embrace this new role of future pastor's wife; I decided I also would try to learn something which was quite Greek to me—the art of how to make what I think is church-people food—a casserole.

Over the years, God has been gracious to slowly unravel me from perfectionism, but as a new wife, in our two-bedroom apartment during our seminary days, I worshiped the idea of appearing perfect to a watching world. I spent most of the day scrubbing the house, vacuuming, dusting the picture frames on the walls, and searching the Internet for a recipe for casseroles.

As I prepared, I was tangled up in the lie that I needed to impress others. I embraced perfectionism and the need to appear as if my home was perfect, while outwardly I fought to feel completely joyful, happy, content, fulfilled, and strong; I couldn't let people see who I really was beneath the surface. In my perfectionism, the real me was afraid to be seen for who I really was, so I layered on falsities to hide my loneliness, fear of the unknown, and insecurities. I layered the idea of looking cleaned up on the outside to prevent anyone from seeing the tangled-up messes which were beneath the surface.

Casseroles were quite Greek to me. My parents were both from the Northeast, and as I was growing up, I don't recall eating many meals called casserole. For some reason, I believed, in order to appear good enough in this Greek-to-me role, I needed to make a casserole on this particular day.

In my limited experience with people whom I had met at church, the after-church party tables were laden with casseroles. Pretty much anything can be made into a casserole. I was fascinated by the many different things one can add to cream of chicken soup, shredded cheddar cheese, sour cream and crushed up crackers. Broccoli, hamburger, corn, chicken, ham, taco, green beans, sweet potatoes, rice, and even a long list of breakfast items can be combined in a 9"x13" casserole dish and baked at 350 degrees.

For me, knowing how to make a proper casserole was a requirement for being a good Christian wife, a requirement I had assigned to myself. I believed I needed "perfect casserole maker" on the resumé I was writing for myself to be seen, known, and accepted as an adequate pastor's wife.

Leading up to this moment, I had zero experience baking a casserole and very little experience with the oven in our two-bedroom apartment. I still am not the best cook, but usually can make something edible when following a recipe. On casserole day, I followed the Internet recipe exactly: preheated the oven; greased the baking dish; cut the chicken breasts into cubes; and mixed together sour cream, sherry cooking wine, cream of chicken soup; topped it with poppy seeds, crushed up Ritz crackers; drizzled it with butter, and then baked it uncovered for fifty minutes.

My house was cleaned to perfection, my casserole was baking in the oven, sweet tea was brewed and chilling, and salad was mixed together. I felt prepared and excited. I couldn't wait to wow and impress our guests with my domestic diva-ing. Beneath the surface I desired to be seen and approved of with my perfect entertaining so much more than I actually desired vulnerable human connection. My cleaned house, pressed outfit, and prepared dinner protected me from being seen as the chaotic, insecure girl I was beneath the shiny surface.

When we sat down for dinner, we prayed with our new friends, and then I served my casserole, the church-people food I was hoping would please the crowd. As I scooped the casserole from the 9"x13" baking dish, what I saw was raw chicken on my serving spoon. My casserole was not cooked perfectly. The chicken was not edible! How could this have happened? I followed the instructions perfectly. I had nothing else to serve and I was completely mortified! Our new friends were gracious and waited with us in my shame-space as I placed the casserole back in the oven. Sadly, in this moment, how well I executed hosting new people in my home as a new wife concerned me more than the actual people around my table. I didn't recover from almost poisoning my guests with raw chicken. Though the night went on, I was completely withdrawn.

While still holding fast to the belief that I needed to appear to be a perfect housewife, ultimately this moment crushed me, but this moment was the beginning of my redemption from perfectionism. My expectation of being a perfectly put together domestic diva and the reality of my domestic disaster collided. I didn't know who I was in failure, and my deeply woven threads of needing to be perfect all the time began to fray.

The Broken Cistern of Perfectionism

What I know now is, in that moment, I didn't know who I was without appearing impressive to others. I am not even sure that in that moment I was able to love myself in a moment of imperfection. Two years after hearing the gospel, that I am a sinner in need of God's grace and mercy which is fully given to me by the atoning blood of Jesus, I stood disappointed over a casserole of raw chicken. Even cognitively knowing the gospel, I was still prone to wander back over to drinking from a broken cistern of muddy stagnant water called perfectionism. The old self was still hanging on and tangled up in the new self. Standing in my dining room laden with disappointment holding an undercooked and imperfect casserole exposed that I still needed God and perfectionism. God alone was not enough for me. I was still prone to wander over to living a life of adding my efforts to the gospel.

The Problem with Perfectionism

Perfectionism is a coping mechanism used to keep us from being vulnerable with others. As long as we can hide beneath a shiny surface, we feel safe behind perfectionism. My husband once had a friend over after class while I was at work. When he told me this after school, I was so angry that he had had a friend over spontaneously simply because I hadn't cleaned the toilets that morning before I went to work. Honestly, I don't think I talked to my husband for a few days over this issue. My anger wasn't about my husband having a friend over, my anger was about letting someone see a side of me that wasn't perfect.

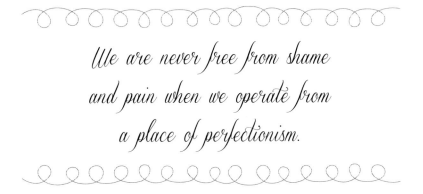

We are never free from shame and pain when we operate from a place of perfectionism.

Slavery to perfection keeps us from unity within the body of Christ. When we desire to show only the most perfect parts of ourselves, we are hindered from the unity Paul writes about in Ephesians 4. Perfectionism prevents us from humility, patience, gentleness, and the ability to bear with one another in love. If we are unable to be patient, humble, gentle, and bear with our own selves in moments of imperfection, how can we extend these things to others within the body of Christ?

Much of my bend toward perfectionism comes from a desire to control. This comes from the deeply-woven threads I have tangled up around my heart in woundedness. I believe if I can show a perfect self, I can protect myself from the deeply-woven shame and pain. We are never free from shame and pain when we operate from a place of perfectionism. Vulnerability is the only thing that can free us from the shame and pain beneath the surface. It is in the human imperfections that God's perfect power is displayed (2 Cor. 12:9).

I have to confess that I find myself back at the broken cistern of perfectionism time and time again. When it comes to perfectionism, I see this cistern as an acceptable sin within the church, so I don't take it too seriously. In perfectionism, I find myself two-stepping between repentance and belief, leaving me tangled up in antinomianism. **Antinomianism** means to be against the law; *anti* meaning against and *nomos* meaning law. In some areas of my life I find myself tangled up in legalism, in some areas I am tangled up in moralism, but when it comes to this sneaky, "not too bad" sin, I leave out the discipline of obedience. I don't try to walk in God's commands to free me from the mask of perfectionism. I find myself tangled up in more false freedom and more grace, failing to apply God's Word to this plaguing part of myself that keeps me from vulnerable community within the church.

When we humbly embrace that we belong to God and are aware of the ungodly desire to only show the most perfect parts of ourselves, then we find ourselves truly free from the yoke of slavery to perfectionism. If we find that we belong to God, we will rest in Christ's perfect work on the cross and surrender our own fallen desires to meaninglessly perfect the world around us. In this world, the greatest commandment is not to have the perfectly decorated home, the tastiest casserole, or a dust-bunny-free hard-wood floor. The greatest commandment is to love God and love others. Slavery to perfectionism prevents us from doing either.

chapter eight

the gospel unravels perfectionism

For at one time you were darkness, but now you are
light in the Lord. Walk as children of light.

EPHESIANS 5:8

Seven years after my shame over the perfect casserole, my husband was the Assistant Pastor of Youth and Children's Ministries at our church in Mason, Ohio. I was eight weeks post-C-section after the birth of our third son. I had three boys three and under in my care as I waved goodbye to Michael when he left a little earlier than I to get to the church for the yearly missions brunch.

I was holding my eight-week-old son, my seventeen-month-old son was in the early stages of walking, and my three-year-old son was quite busy and into everything. Part of attending the missions brunch was to bring a casserole to share with others. I had made a requirement for myself that as one of the pastors' wives, I must bring a casserole. I could barely care for myself in the season of having three boys three and under but ruled by fear and under the yoke of slavery to perfectionism, I made a requirement for myself that the youth pastor's wife must show up to the brunch with a casserole in hand.

Once again, I found my expectations and realities colliding.

I was running late and pulled the casserole out of the oven ten minutes before I needed to be through the doors of our church and in the sanctuary. I burnt my hands moving the casserole from the oven and into its carry bag, and then angrily loaded my babies into the minivan—all because of my slavery to perfectionism. Again, I found tension between the kind of woman I was and how well I could execute showing up to a church function appearing rested, joyous, and casseroled. Painfully, I took out my frustration with my shortcomings by being impatient with my children.

I was already exhausted by the time I arrived at church. The stress, the loading and unloading of three small children in and out of the van, and the casserole all were physically taking a toll on my eight-week post-C-section body.

At this point in my life, I pushed a stroller the size of an eighteen-wheeler—a double-wide, side-by-side City Mini with an infant car seat attachment for my eight-week-old, a seat for my seventeen-month-old, and a kickboard on the back where my three-year-old could stand and ride. I loaded my kids in the truck-sized double stroller and carefully balanced my breakfast casserole in the basket beneath the stroller for the short stroll through what was now a parking lot filled with cars but emptied of people. I was late, as usual, and though surrounded by my family and a community of believers, I felt alone. Alone in the parking lot, I was just one "how are you doing" away from tears, but I chose to hide behind an "I'm fine" smile. In unbelief, I felt God needed me to appear as if I could do it all.

At the missions brunch, I found myself trying to hide near the back of the room. I hid because I feared letting others really see I was on the brink of tears. I was not strong in that moment. I was weak, but behind perfection, I could hide. While I retreated back into my shame spaces in the back of the sanctuary, God sent someone to speak truth to me. Despite my effort to hide, I was pursued. This friend asked me how I was, and I immediately began to cry. She then asked me, "Rachel, why didn't you just forget about the casserole? What if you just showed up empty-handed?"

Once again, this idea of what I felt like I had to be collided with reality, and what was beneath the surface of my heart was exposed. Even after all this time, I still didn't know who I was with empty hands. I still didn't know how to operate in imperfection or in moments when I came without anything to offer. I still needed to appear perfectly put together to a watching world, because deep down, I did not believe I was enough when my hands were empty. I did not believe I am enough when I can't measure up to the expectations I have for myself as a mother, wife, friend, and pastor's wife.

The gospel calls us to die to ourselves. We cannot when we lack self-awareness of what lies beneath the surface of our hearts.

Perfectionism, Fear, and Control

> There is no fear in love, but perfect love casts out fear.
> For fear has to do with punishment, and whoever
> fears has not been perfected in love. — 1 JOHN 4:18

Struggles with perfectionism come from a tangled-up understanding of strength and identity. The tangled-up view to appear perfect is related to the fear of being seen and known in one's knobbly skins. Perfectionism allows us to control what we allow into our worlds; this control protects us from the deep pain tangled up beneath the surface. All of the threads of perfection and control are gospel issues deeply woven in fear. This could be the fear of losing again, the fear of hurting again, the fear of the shame felt for being less than perfect. When we walk in the appearance of human perfection, we are not walking as someone who has been made perfect in love; living life behind the mask of perfection prohibits us in the body to have vulnerable human connection, keeps us in slavery to our pride, and leaves parts of ourselves tangled up in the darkness which Christ has redeemed us from.

The first step in unraveling yourself from perfectionism and control is to become aware of your heart's bend towards them. The best way to guard your heart against its bend to perfection is to know your heart well, to become an expert in the gospel-centered desires of your heart aligned with God's Word as well as an expert in the man-centered distorted desires of your heart tangled up in pride and the sinful nature. The gospel calls us to die to ourselves. We cannot die to ourselves when we lack self-awareness of what lies beneath the surface of our hearts.

> Above all else, guard your heart, for everything you do flows from it. — PROVERBS 4:23 (NIV)

Perfecting Conversations

Have you ever rehearsed a conversation in your head over and over again? I have left Bible Study on several mornings with four children, and on our short drive home, I have over-rehearsed the conversations I had during the discussion times. Instead of seeing Jesus and leaving Bible Study with a full heart, at times I find myself picking apart conversations to perfect them to the way I think they should have gone. In my thought-life this sounds like: "If I would have said this, maybe she wouldn't have thought I meant that" or the extreme, "Next time I just won't say anything at all." My desire to perfect myself takes over my thought life; this kind of perfection-ism causes me to continue to wander over to the broken cisterns of approval, acceptance, and control that I have. There are so many layers to my "if I could, then I could" problems.

> We destroy arguments and every lofty opinion raised against the knowledge of God and take every thought captive to obey Christ. — 2 CORINTHIANS 10:5

When I perfect conversations in my thought life, I am trying to control instead of resting in the gospel-security I have in Jesus and His work on the cross. Jesus died for my imperfections. If I fumbled in one of my Bible Study answers or felt misunderstood in a conversation, Jesus and His power are perfectly displayed even in my shortcomings. I can rest in the words I have said that may have not come out perfectly.

Transforming the way you think about yourself and others is necessary in the Christian life.

Learning from my imperfect words and embracing wisdom is very different than dwelling on moments of imperfectly spoken words. Satan and his schemes have a sneaky way to pull on my threads of unbelief when I am perfecting conversations. Fear takes over in these moments, and I find myself stepping away from vulnerable community and back into my shame spaces. In the darkness of an unredeemed thought-life ruled by perfectionism, Satan has the power, even the power to sometimes cause me to withdraw from others.

When I find myself overthinking conversations, one thing I do is talk to myself, instead of listening to myself. As crazy as it sounds, reminding myself of truth out loud destroys the power of the devil in my thought-life because it brings the darkness of my unredeemed thoughts into the light. Transforming the way you think about yourself and others is necessary in the Christian life.

> Do not be conformed to this world, but be transformed by the renewal of your mind, that by testing

you may discern what is the will of God, what is good
and acceptable and perfect. — ROMANS 12:2

Perfecting one's thought-life and past conversations has to unravel away in the gospel. Overthinking can easily turn into control
and fear instead of faith and trust. As women being redeemed by
Christ and His work on the cross, we must take our thoughts captive,
repent of our tendencies to perfect our words in our thought-life
rehearsal, be transformed by talking to ourselves with truth when
we see ourselves walking towards the darkness of perfecting past
conversations, and believe that God is pleased with us even in our
imperfections; He is making us new.

> Finally, brothers, whatever is true, whatever is honor-
> able, whatever is just, whatever is pure, whatever
> is lovely, whatever is commendable, if there is any
> excellence, if there is anything worthy of praise,
> think about these things. — PHILIPPIANS 4:8

God's Provision Is Outside of Human Control

After our time at the church-planting assessment center, Michael
told me he felt God was calling him to stay at North Cincinnati
Community Church and possibly be the lead pastor there one
day. I said, "Okay, I hear you, but we need to be intentional about
a back-up plan because God won't call you to be the next lead
pastor at North Cincinnati Community Church." At the time
our current lead pastor had been serving at North Cincinnati for
twenty years, and I didn't think he would retire for several more
years, while we were ready for a change to happen within a two-
year time span.

Four months after assessment center, we put our house on
the market and were considering renting a home as we pursued
church-planting internships as well as a few other job openings
in all parts of the country. We thought if our house sold quickly,
maybe this would be affirmation that God was calling us to move.
I was eight weeks pregnant and nauseous with our fourth child, I

had three boys under four running around our small home, and I was cleaning out and staging our house to be shown to potential buyers. The day we put our house on the market, the founding and lead pastor of North Cincinnati Community Church shared with our session his plan for retirement and succession. The day we put our house on the market, the session approached Michael to be a candidate for the lead pastor position. To my surprise, the one thing I thought God wouldn't do was happening. Our house sold by-owner after twenty-four hours on the market. We received three offers on our home, all above asking price.

I felt very much out of control during this time; this was not a part of the plan I was personally writing for my family. It was an honor for Michael to be asked to be a candidate for the role of lead pastor at North Cincinnati Community Church, but deep down, because of my threads of unbelief, I still did not believe God was calling us to stay. Staying near my hometown road and settling into a permanent role would cause me to have to continue to face the demons of my past, especially if Michael were called to serve as the lead pastor at North Cincinnati Community Church.

As a perfectionist, this waiting space was a difficult place to walk through. For our protection, there was not a lot of communication from the session or the pastor search committee, and God put me in a waiting space where I was completely out of control. I trained for and ran my first half-marathon during that time, as well as cleaned and scrubbed a lot of grout in our bathrooms. For eighteen months I could not perfect or control the future for my family. There wasn't a task I could complete to move the process along more quickly or an accolade I could show the session and the pastor search committee to prove we were the worthy candidate. In that eighteen-month season, God was just calling me to be still and to wait. As a woman who is highly task-orientated, being still was a radical way for me to live.

Be still, and know that I am God. — PSALM 46:10

I struggled during this season of waiting and I wrestled with my heart. At times, my unhealthy threads woven around my wounds, lies, and vows caused me to leave my Bible Study. I feared speaking up during the prayer requests to make known to others that I was not waiting well. I feared this because I believed my difficulty with being still in this waiting space would reflect poorly on my husband and his ministry. So, because of fear, I suffered in silence, and this drove me away from community.

I ran three to four times a week in that season, and I preferred to run alone. It was painful to unravel alone in the waiting space; honestly, in that season I wasn't sure who was for me and who was against me. This was a sticky place for me to wrestle with my shame and feelings of not-enoughness, but what God taught me in this season was that I was still struggling beneath the surface. I was still tangled-up in the slavery of performance-based living. This was another layer for me to unravel. I do not have to be enough. God is enough. His ways are sometimes not understandable, but His ways and His timing are good. I can trust Him even with empty hands.

> Trust in the Lord with all your heart, and do not lean on your own understanding. In all your ways acknowledge him, and he will make straight your paths. — PROVERBS 3:5-6

Letting Go of Control

As I was putting the finishing touches on this book, I also went on my first mission trip with our church to Croatia. As a perfectionist, I am perfectly content to live each day the same exact way. My perfectionist heart loves the predictability and the control I have when each day can run in the same exact way as the day before. When I was approached to go on this trip to Croatia, I wanted to go, but the perfectionist inside of me struggled with the uncertainty and the unknowns of our being away from our four children, halfway across the world, for eleven days.

Our church has been traveling to serve in Croatia for twenty years, and over the years this trip has become known for unpredictability, so much so that the trip to Croatia is also called "Flexatia."

Now, I still order chicken nuggets, french fries, a coke without ice, and a variety of sauces at McDonalds as a thirty-five-year-old because I like to keep things the same. Unpredictability, change, unknowns, and "flexatia-ing" are all words that cause intense feelings of anxiety. Leaving my nice cozy life in the suburbs of Ohio, letting go of the control of my children, and letting go of the control over my own schedule were challenging for me.

One day I spent too much time listening to myself in my unredeemed thoughts, and I thought about how I was going to die while I was in Croatia and my children would become orphans. I spent the morning crying and writing letters to each of my children in case I were to pass away during my trip to Croatia. Another day, I thought about my children drowning in the pool while I was away, and I thought about my home catching on fire in the middle of the night and how I wasn't sure if all of the children were completely aware of my fire evacuation plan. I left a twenty-four-page manual on how to care for my children while I was away, including detailed instructions on how to make a quesadilla for my brother, who happens to be a chef. I planned out almost every moment for my children while I was away, because of my fear, perfectionism, and control. With my mouth I say I believe God is in control, but in the unknowns, I don't always trust Him. I am in slavery to my fear when I fail to believe that God cares for me and my children much more than I ever could. There are so many layers I have to unravel when it comes to perfectionism and control.

I went to Croatia one baby-step at a time, and God provided. He provided aunts, uncles, and cousins to stay at my home with my children; He provided friends to pick my children up and take them for play dates; He provided church family to sit with my children during the two Sundays we were away from church; He provided almost 100% of the finances for me to fly to Croatia through the financial giving of my friends.

One baby-step at a time I said goodbye to my children, I walked to the car, I rode to the airport, I boarded one plane, then another, then another. Each moment was challenging, but because I desire to unravel in the freedom of the gospel from my perfectionist and controlling tendencies, I went to Croatia and I fought to trust God to continue to provide while I was away— and He did. The blessings I received when I took small steps of faith outside my comfort and control, were more blessings than I could have ever asked for or thought up. I taught gospel-centered memory verses for five days to one hundred elementary-aged children, I connected with an age-diverse team from our church and now have a sweet connection to each of them, and I made sweet life-long friendships with the men and women at Mačkovec Baptist Church.

> Now to him who is able to do far more abundantly
> than all that we ask or think, according to the power
> at work within us, to him be glory in the church and
> in Christ Jesus throughout all generations, forever and
> ever. Amen. — EPHESIANS 3:20-21

When I returned from Croatia, I came home to my home and children looking the same way they did when I left, and I repented that I spent so much energy worrying over the things that were outside of my control. My time in Croatia is a part of the unraveling of perfectionism and control in my story. God showed up even when my faith was smaller than a mustard seed, and now I long to go back to Mačkovec, Croatia and reconnect with the new family God has given me half-way across the world.

Are You a Slave to Perfectionism?

Questions to assess how perfectionism may impact your personal life:

- Do you find yourself saying yes to too many things?

- Do you have higher expectations for yourself than you do for others?

- Are you easily frustrated when things do not go the way you expected them to go? Is there a critical voice in your consciousness which feels louder at times when you stumble?

- Do you leave a conversation and then are occupied by things you should have said? Does this rehearsal of the conversation keep you preoccupied in your thoughts?

These questions will help you assess if perfectionism is preventing you from vulnerable community with others:

- Do you find the critical voice in your head speaking when you notice imperfection in others?

- Are you quick to point out and correct the imperfections in the lives of those around you?

- Do you fail to see others as in process in the gospel?

- Do other people know the real you or just the perfected parts of you?

- Do you care how others see you more than you care about your position in Christ?

- Does your need to do things right keep you from stepping out in the community of faith within the church?

- Do you assume others have high expectations for you? Your parenting? Your Sunday School answers?

- Are you reluctant to jump into community in the church because you fear you are not enough or not ready?

Freedom to Have Empty Hands

"What if I just showed up empty-handed?" My friend's powerful words from that missions conference years ago have moved my heart to consider freedom from perfection. They have probed my heart, and finally, now I am beginning to see myself as enough, even with empty hands. The freedom found in the gospel has unraveled how I think about casseroles, empty hands, and perfectionism. I have had to completely lay down all the things I want to perfect at the foot of the cross. It is a sweet unraveling reminder to me that I don't control the world and I don't have to perfect every tiny box. God holds up the world and He is writing a good redemptive story for me as I learn to trust in Him.

Walking with Jesus is a constant waltz. It is a constant putting off of the old ways, turning from them, being renewed in your mind, and walking in the new ways of Jesus, free from the yoke of slavery called perfectionism.

I am not a fully-recovered perfectionist yet; I am still in the process of the slow unraveling of the old self. Now, eleven years from the two-bedroom apartment in St. Louis and an under-cooked casserole—even though I am more experienced in baking casseroles—I don't always sign up to bring one. Sometimes when hosting new people in my home, I serve hot dogs and potato chips from a bag. This is not because I cannot cook, but because I'd rather serve something low-maintenance, so I can focus on the people I am hosting instead of fussing over tasks and food. The self-awareness of this desire to perfect and control is a step in the right direction of being free from feeling like I need to be perfect before a watching world.

Once the monster called perfectionism is on my radar, I am able to ask God to help unravel the threads of perfectionism from my patchwork. I am also able to invite others into my life to keep me accountable in guarding my heart from perfectionism. Through hot dogs, showing up empty-handed, and trusting that I don't control the world, the unraveling of the old and its passing away bring freedom and rest from the yoke of the slavery of impressing and controlling others. Now, so many years later, this perfectionism monster still haunts me, but because I can recognize her, I also know how to battle her a little bit better.

It is only in this newfound freedom that I can see my true self, untethered from all those false layers of wanting to impress and control a watching world. Now I find I am freer to embrace the woman God has made me to be, and truly, this draws me closer to new friends than a perfectly cooked casserole or my perfectly laid plans ever could. It is only through bare-boned vulnerability, in the freedom from perfectionism, that we can move toward others and love well.

Walking with Jesus is a constant waltz. It is a constant putting off of the old ways, turning from them, being renewed in your mind, and walking in the new ways of Jesus, free from the yoke of slavery called perfectionism. With each layer of old that unravels away, I find the woman God is making me to be in Christ. This woman is a recovering perfectionist, mostly likable by humans, but she is deeply loved by God whether she serves a perfectly cooked casserole or feels out of control when timelines and seasons don't go just as she perfectly planned them to go.

Come to me, all you who labor and are heavy laden,
and I will give you rest. Take my yoke upon you,
and learn from me, for I am gentle and lowly in heart,
and you will find rest for your souls.
For my yoke is easy, and my burden is light.

MATTHEW 11:28-30

part four

marriage

chapter nine

the gospel unravels communication and conflict in marriage

Wives, submit to your own husbands, as to the Lord.
For the husband is the head of the wife even as Christ is
the head of the church, his body, and is himself its Savior.
Now as the church submits to Christ, so also wives
should submit in everything to their husbands.
Husbands, love your wives, as Christ loved the church
and gave himself up for her, that he might sanctify her,
having cleansed her by the washing of water with the word,
so that he might present the church to himself in splendor,
without spot or wrinkle or any such thing, that she
might be holy and without blemish. In the same way
husbands should love their wives as their own bodies.
He who loves his wife loves himself. For no one ever hated
his own flesh, but nourishes and cherishes it, just as Christ
does the church, because we are members of his body.

EPHESIANS 5:22-30

99

*R*ecently, I participated in an exercise on expectations vs. realities. The presenter gave each woman a piece of paper with two lines on it. On the top line we were asked to plot how we had imagined our lives would go when we were around the age of sixteen. On the bottom line, we were to plot how our lives actually turned out. What was eye opening to me was that of all the women in my group, I was the only one, who, as a teenager, never saw myself getting married or having children. As a teenager, I always desired to go to college, become successful, live in the big city, and live alone. If I did see myself having children, it was by adopting one after I had become successful. I had seen my life turning out similar to the plot line of the 1987 film *Baby Boom*.

God calls us to live in unity with others, with all humility and gentleness, bearing with one another in love. This unity starts at home in our marriages.

My grief and the unhealthy threads I had woven around my heart affected the way I had seen my future life, my ability to love others, and my worthiness for marriage and family life. Embracing the unhealthy threads of control and self-protection, I never desired marriage and family. I lived with the tangled-up belief that if I could protect myself from establishing a family, I could protect myself from the pain of losing a family member again. As a teenager and college student, I was involved in committed relationships, but deep down, in the threads I had woven, I struggled with commitment issues rooted in fear. I never believed I was worthy of being loved (an unraveling-tangled-up view of my identity); I didn't want to be known in my knobbly skins, so I hid behind a mask (a tangled view of strength); and I couldn't love myself or others with imperfections (control and perfectionism sabotaged intimacy).

God has a funny way of unraveling the tangled-up ways in which we see the world. One year after I understood the gospel for the first time with spiritual ears, I began dating Michael. The length of time between the first time we met to our wedding day was less than a year. Then, beginning in 2009, God gave us four children in four years. By the time I was thirty years old, I was not living in the big city all alone over a carton of Chinese take-out. By the age of thirty, I was married with four kids four and under, living back near my hometown, and married to a pastor.

I am grateful for how God has written my story. My husband and each of my children are blessings I believed I never deserved, but my husband and my children are exactly what I needed to help redeem me from my shame-spaces and feelings of unworthiness. I have not done marriage well; each day has been an opportunity for me to gospel waltz away from old patterns, have the eyes of my heart enlightened by God's power working within me, and walk in new patterns woven in the Word of God.

God has used the gift of marriage to teach me the simple truth that we are not called to live behind massive walls of self-protection or hide in our shame-spaces. We are called to live in vulnerable community with others. God calls us to live in unity with others, with all humility and gentleness, bearing with one another in love. This unity starts at home in our marriages. It is no accident the book of Ephesians is written in the order it is written in. It is quite necessary to have a clear picture of the gospel before you can dance well in marriage.

In Ephesians 1, we see Who created us and what we were created for, the access we have to the glorious riches of His grace, the hope we have been called to, and the greatness of power working in and through us. In chapter two, we are reminded that we have been called to live out the gospel not because of anything we do, but because of who God is. Chapter two reminds us that we were dead before we understood the truth of the gospel with spiritual ears, but God has made us alive. God is making all of us alive in Christ, both those who were far off and those who were near. In chapter three, we see the exhortation to be renewed in our hearts, to be transformed in our inner being so we can know the height and breadth of the love of Christ. It is not until a person can grasp this gospel-centered identity that she can be called to live in unity with others inside the church. Chapter four is the urgency of unity, by the unraveling of the old, the renewal of patterns, and the embracing of walking in new patterns. Then, here in chapter five we find how we are called to live out unity in covenantal marriage. Without gospel-centered identity, it is impossible to live out gospel-centered unity in marriage.

A Tangled-Up View of Strength Impacts Marriage

I remember our pre-engagement counseling very clearly. During the first session, we completed a fill-in-the-blank about the gospel. "God is more **sovereign**, **holy** and **powerful** than you can comprehend, you are more **sinful**, **wretched** and **evil** than you can understand, but at the same time, in Christ, you are more **forgiven**, **loved** and **blameless** than you can dare to believe" (adapted from Timothy Keller's definition of the gospel in *The Meaning of Marriage*).[1] This promise has greatly impacted the way I see myself in my marriage. I love my husband very much, but I am not able to love him well until I can first step out of the shame-spaces God is calling me to step out of in the gospel. When I don't see the gospel in focus, I cannot live as a healthy, gospel-centered Christian in marriage.

Before I met my husband, I lived behind large walls of self-protection. I believed weakness and vulnerability were the farthest things from being a strong woman. I was independent, I did not want to answer to anyone—I was quite the typical girl-boss. The last thing I had ever been to anyone was submissive. Before I heard the gospel of grace with spiritual ears, the only person I ever wanted to be accountable to was myself. Being accountable to others is a deeply woven heart struggle for me. The words from Ephesians 5, "*wives submit to your husbands,*" still send a wave of

---

1   Timothy Keller, *The Meaning of Marriage: Facing the Complexities of Commitment with the Wisdom of God* (New York: Penguin Group, 2011), 46.

prickles across my heart. I need to constantly be unraveling the way I used to live to the way God is calling me to live in marriage.

For me, when I first met Michael, I desired to be led by him because he was a godly leader. However, the words from Ephesians 5 about submitting to my husband rubbed up against the way I had always lived my life. It is in marriage that God unraveled me from the way I used to see myself and helped me embrace Christian community, the gospel, vulnerability, freedom from shame, and the courage to be fully seen and loved, not for who I have been in my shame-spaces, but seen and loved for the person God is making me to be in the gospel.

I submit to my husband out of a reverence to Christ because my life is no longer my own (Galatians 2:20).

Old Identity Binds Us to Slavery

As a new wife, I easily forgot the gospel. The word *submit* rubbed me the wrong way when I saw myself in my old identity. For me, submitting to my husband has been a supernatural power, not an easily learned behavior. Even when I have outwardly submitted to my husband, I have found myself living with bitterness beneath the surface. God has had to unravel me from my old patterns of self-centeredness, so I could learn to live in gospel-centered community with my husband in marriage. When I see submission to my husband as being out of reverence to the Lord, that is the only time I find myself gospel-waltzing well in marriage. The verse directly before these well-known words from Ephesians on marriage (5:21) says "submitting to one another out of a reverence to the Lord." I submit to my husband out of a reverence to Christ

103

because my life is no longer my own (Gal. 2:20).

The word submission in our culture has a negative connotation associated with weakness, but submission simply means *to come under*. Just like I come under the care and authority of God, or the care and authority of the church, I come under the care and authority of my husband. The word submission and its negative connotation in the world is unraveled in the gospel in the same way my tangled-up view of strength was unraveled in the gospel. Submission is evidence of a life unraveled and an act of worship to the One who delivered my life from total darkness and transferred me to His heavenly kingdom where I have redemption, the forgiveness of sins (Col. 1:13-14). It is impossible to see myself rightly in covenantal marriage if I forget the Holy Spirit is in me, and the same power that raised Christ from the dead is slowly redeeming my unhealthy threads. That same power is within me daily, so I can die to my old patterns and be raised up to walk in new gospel-centered patterns.

I also want to repeat this here: *we submit to one another out of a reverence to Christ*. Biblical submission is beautiful and reflects the loving relationship between God the Father and God the Son. Jesus submitted to the will of His Father. It is biblical that Jesus and the Father both have different functions within the Trinity, and it is biblical that men and women have different functions within the context of marriage. When thinking biblically, we see that male and female are created with the same importance, honor, and dignity, but their roles are different. This is called **complementarianism**. Complementarianism simply means males and females are created to have different attributes and gifts, and those attributes and gifts complement one another.

Biblical submission out of a reverence to Christ never condones anything that is not biblical. Biblical submission never submits to sin; this means women are not called to come under leadership that abuses, is addicting, or is adulterous. Yes, we are called to forgive as Christ has forgiven us, but we should never continue to submit in relationships which painfully continue to abuse, manipulate, or cause us to be physically harmed. Men who follow Christ should be displaying Christ-like character that reflects the character of biblical manhood. They should honor women, provide protection and safety for women, and encourage women to use their complementary gifts for the building up of the home and the church. Karen Hodge and Susan Hunt in *Life-Giving Leadership* also note, "Submission is not a one-time event; it is a daily submitting our glory to God's glory. It is evidence of His life in us and the expression of our love for the One who first loved us."[2] Submission is a constant invitation to daily unravel in the gospel.

> So if there is any encouragement in Christ, any comfort from love, any participation in the Spirit, any affection and sympathy, complete my joy by being of the same mind, having the same love, being in full accord and of one mind. Do nothing from selfish ambition or conceit, but in humility count others more significant than yourselves. Let each of you look not only to his own interests, but also to the interests of others. Have this mind among yourselves, which is yours in Christ Jesus, who, though he was in the form of God, did not count equality with God a thing to be grasped, but emptied himself, by taking the form of a servant, being born in the likeness of men. And being found in human form, he humbled himself by becoming obedient to the point of death, even death on a cross. Therefore God has highly exalted him and bestowed on him the name that is above every name, so that at the name of Jesus every knee should bow, in heaven and on earth and under the earth, and every tongue confess that Jesus Christ is Lord, to the glory of God the Father. — PHILIPPIANS 2:1-11

---

2   Karen Hodge and Susan Hunt, *Life-giving Leadership* (Lawrenceville, Georgia: Committee on Discipleship Ministries, 2018), 92.

Personality Differences, Communication and Reverence

The tension of old and new threads in covenantal marriage has been sweet but tough. It is a heart struggle to extend the gospel of grace to my own heart, let alone extend the gospel of grace to my husband in marriage. Marriage has been a tough place for me to learn how to live in unity with someone who has been woven together differently than God has woven me. The toughness has not been tough in a way that is agonizing but, instead, irritating. This irritation has been enough to rub up against my old patterns, just enough for me to feel the tension between a life lived centered around self and a life centered around others in gospel community.

I love my husband, and we have an aligned vision for how we want to invest our lives and raise our children, but in the first few weeks of marriage we both discovered . . . communication is a difficult place for us. Those words from our pre-engagement counseling about being sinful and blameless at the same time were needed within the first few weeks of marriage when we found ourselves speaking "Venus" and "Mars" languages—me fired up with emotion and him with a logical answer and a fix for every situation.

> Marriage is the union of two people who arrive toting the luggage of life. And that luggage always contains sin. — **Dave Harvey**, *When Sinners Say "I Do": Discovering the Power of the Gospel for Marriage* [3]

Our sin-filled luggage was present in those first weeks in our first two-bedroom apartment, but we didn't really discover we were toting that luggage around until we walked into a professor's office at Covenant Theological Seminary for our initial, mandatory meeting as a couple for a class called Spiritual and Ministry Formation. In this meeting, we as a couple had our very first "ah-ha" moment as to why we had both been missing one another so often in the arena of communication.

---

3   Dave Harvey, *When Sinners Say "I Do": Discovering the Power of the Gospel for Marriage* (Wapwallopen, PA: Shepherd Press, 2007), 15.

After several assessments, I was given my results of the Myers-Brigg Personality Test as an ESFJ, Extroverted, Sensing (detail-focused), Feeling, Judging; and Michael tested as an ENTJ, Extroverted, Intuitive (big picture-focused), Thinking, Judging. When the professor plotted our two personalities, he winced. Through pursed lips the professor said, "Ooooooooh." Then there was a long pause before he concluded with, "I see ... you may have some communication issues."

Our personalities were plotted on opposite sides of the Myers-Brigg temperament wheel. Michael and I both process outwardly in the same way with our extroversion and judging, but the way we communicate and process our inner worlds is completely different. I process the world through feelings, details, and feelings of those details, and Michael processes the world through his thoughts, logic, and seeing the big picture.

Basically, when I searched the Internet for the kind of spouse I should be looking for based on the Myers-Brigg Personality Test, what I discovered was that ESFJs and ENTJs are the least likely to be compatible. They are not just on opposite sides of the plotting wheel, they are on wince-level sides of the plotting wheel. Communication was a hot mess for us in our early years of marriage. This was so challenging for me as a new Christian in Christian marriage! For some reason, I lived with the tangled-up belief that if I cognitively knew the gospel, Jesus would bless me with a conflict-free marriage.

God made Michael and me both unique for His glory. I believe it is quite a beautiful thing for God to unite two completely different people together in covenantal marriage. The unraveling of my old patterns of communicating out of my woundedness has been necessary for gospel-centered unity in my marriage. This unraveling of my communication patterns is the manifestation of Christ in me, the hope of glory. It is proof of a life being redeemed by Jesus, out of reverence for Christ. I submit to my husband and humbly die to myself as we learn how to gospel waltz in communication.

Self-protection, shame, unworthiness, and perfection have all tangled up the way I think about communication. For most of my life before Christ, I lived a life where conflict was ignored instead of worked through. It was better to not say anything at all than to speak up and say something. I learned to never express feelings which were negative out of fear of being seen as less than perfect and a fear of emotional abandonment if I were seen in my knobbly skins.

After our first big argument—most likely over vacuum lines in the carpet or water glasses on the kitchen countertop—I found myself hurt because my husband would not bend towards my slavery to perfection. My self-centeredness in this moment clouded my judgment, and I was unable to see any other way to vacuum the carpet other than my own.

In my woundedness, I found myself embracing my old patterns of communication. I found myself shutting down, stone-walling, and hiding my hurts behind the closed door of my bedroom. When it came to conflict, shutting down and hiding were the only behaviors I knew.

Once Michael began to see me shutting down and retreating into my shame-spaces, and as a good husband, he came to me and sat down beside me on our blue-checkered loveseat. Then he opened his Bible to Ephesians 5 and asked me to discuss our conflict with him and pray that God would help us in that moment. I knew the words from Ephesians 5. I had memorized them, but with my self-centered ways, I did not want to be reminded of the words of Ephesians 5. The way I was behaving and the words I confessed to believe in rubbed against one another.

Sitting next to my new husband, with my personal luggage of sin patterns woven in self-centeredness, self-protection and even self-pity, I was not able to unravel my old self. Without the unraveling of the old self, I was unable to put off my old patterns of dealing with conflict and walk in the newness of life by applying God's Word in that heated moment over vacuum lines. I remember looking at Michael in that moment when I was so hot with emotion, and I hissed at him, "You get that Bible away from me." In my self-centeredness I could not see what the gospel had to do with our fight over vacuuming lines.

In that moment, I was not ready to hear the Truth, the Truth that Michael and I, both of us—out of a reverence for Christ, because Christ had laid His life down for us—needed to lay down our pride for one another—even in the simplicity of laying down the detail of how one believes vacuum lines should look. Submitting to my husband is not weakness as the world would define it, submitting is loving and respecting selflessly out of a spiritual love for Christ. I knew this truth on a cognitive level when we lived in our two-bedroom apartment in St. Louis, but I fell so short when it came to the application of this truth in my life. When it came to walking in my heavenly shoes and submitting to my husband out of reverence to the Lord, I needed not just a behavior pattern to help me be more submissive, I needed a change in my inner self that would cause me to love Jesus and follow His Truth, even when my heart was so tangled up in emotion.

When the googly-eyed goggles came off just a few weeks into our marriage, we both began to see each other through the true lens of the Scripture. I was a sinner, wound up in my old patterns, and my husband was a sinner wound up in his. We were at the same time more sinful than we could imagine, and, in Christ, more blameless and forgiven than we could even dare to hope. We both needed to begin to work hard to see one another through the lens of the gospel. In his book, *The Meaning of Marriage: Facing the Complexities of Commitment with the Wisdom of God*, Tim Keller defines the gospel this way: "The gospel is this: We are more sinful and flawed in ourselves than we ever dared believe, yet at the very same time we are more loved and accepted in Jesus Christ than we ever dared hope." [4]

In the first weeks of marriage I believed I was sinful and I believed Michael was flawed, but I didn't believe we were *that* sinful and flawed. I certainly didn't soak in the truth that we both were more sinful and flawed than I dared to believe. I absolutely hadn't reached the (Bloom's Taxonomy) level of synthesizing this truth through God's greater redemptive story: *at the very same time* we are more loved and accepted in Jesus than we ever dared to hope. I know this because I did not live out this freedom with humility.

Michael and I both had so much unraveling to do. In Christian

---

4   Timothy Keller, *The Meaning of Marriage: Facing the Complexities of Commitment with the Wisdom of God*, 46.

marriage, it is a blessing and a privilege to look at a sinner-spouse whose sin is rubbing up against you just enough to irritate your skin and give you contact dermatitis, to look at that spouse and feel the irritation of sin and yet, at the very same time, choose to see him with the eyes of Jesus, more loved and accepted in Jesus than you can dare to hope. To choose to extend mercy and grace to your spouse is an application of believing the truth of the gospel; extending mercy and grace is how we show our spouses the love of Jesus on this earth. This is an intentional practice that requires knowing that both you and your spouse are more sinful and flawed than you ever dared to believe, *yet at the very same time* you are more loved and accepted than you ever dared to hope. Automatically extending mercy and grace is the fruit of walking in truth. This takes spiritual transformation through prayer and the Holy Spirit, because walking in love, joy, peace, patience, kindness, goodness, faithfulness, gentleness, and self-control are spiritual things. Extending mercy and grace to those who have rubbed you the wrong way is not the way of this world. The extension of mercy and grace to sinners who have done nothing but leave you irritated or even wounded are the ways of Jesus. Mercy and grace, laying down your pride, and unraveling your old patterns to walk in the newness you have in Christ show evidence and fruit that you are no longer of this world, that your citizenship is a heavenly one.

> When your ears hear and your eyes see the sin, weakness, or failure of your husband or wife, it is never an accident; it is always grace. God loves your spouse, and he is committed to transforming him or her by his grace, and he has chosen you to be one of his regular tools of change. — **Paul David Tripp**, *What Did You Expect?: Redeeming the Realities of Marriage*[5]

I think communication and conflict resolution wouldn't have been as difficult in those early days of marriage if I had taken Ephesians 4:22-24 more seriously, if I would have thought about

---

5 Paul David Tripp, *What Did You Expect?: Redeeming the Realities of Marriage* (Wheaton, IL: Crossway, 2010), 24.

the gospel more deeply and cared more about seeing my spouse with the eyes of Jesus and walking in the shoes of my heavenly citizenship, the shoes of mercy and grace. I do not think it is an accident at all that the words of putting off the old self and putting on the new self, created after the likeness of God in true righteousness and holiness, come right before the words of Ephesians 5 with instructions for loving your spouse. This is something I still don't do perfectly; I still have so much more unraveling to do, but God has used my marriage to Michael for me to experience the true beauty of Christian marriage. To have someone who loves me not for who I am now, but who loves me for the woman God is unraveling me to be in Jesus through this process of putting off the old and walking in new heavenly shoes.

Mercy and grace, laying down your pride, and unraveling your old patterns to walk in the newness you have in Christ show evidence and fruit that you are no longer of this world, that your citizenship is a heavenly one.

Unraveling my communication patterns out of reverence to Christ has been necessary for me in marriage. I have needed to unravel my old patterns—the desire to hide behind shutting down and stonewalling others—when it comes to communication and resolving conflict. This has required a renewal of my inner self and a fight to believe that God's Spirit is renewing me in the spirit of my mind. It is not until I am aware of these old patterns that I am able to step out of them and walk in obedience by putting on the new self, created out of true righteousness and holiness. Transforming the way I communicate with my spouse out of a reverence for Christ helps me to see my husband as God sees him. Even when I feel he is being wretched, sinful, and evil, in the gospel I can choose to see him as fully loved, completely blameless, and totally forgiven in Christ. This extension of mercy to my husband is a display of the same love and forgiveness God has given to me in Christ.

Learning to waltz has caused Michael and me both to have a few bruised toes along the way, but in the bruising while we learn to dance, we step out of superficial love for one another and learn to love in the way that God loves. "To be loved but not known is comforting but superficial. To be known and not loved is our greatest fear. But to be fully known and truly loved is, well, a lot like being loved by God. It is what we need more than anything. It liberates us from pretense, humbles us out of our self-righteousness, and fortifies us for any difficulty life can throw at us." [6]

---

6   Timothy Keller, *The Meaning of Marriage: Facing the Complexities of Commitment with the Wisdom of God*, 95.

chapter ten

the gospel unravels expectations in marriage

"Therefore a man shall leave his father and mother and
hold fast to his wife, and the two shall become one flesh."
This mystery is profound, and I am saying
that it refers to Christ and the church. However,
let each one of you love his wife as himself,
and let the wife see that she respects her husband.

EPHESIANS 5:31-33

ave Harvey in his book, *When Sinners Say I Do*, writes,
"Marriage is the union of two people who arrive toting
the luggage of life. And that luggage always contains sin."[1] The
luggage of our lives contains the stories of who we are, and
carrying it into marriage means when we come to marriage, we
are bringing expectations, whether we are aware of this or not.
All of us bring family patterns, communication patterns, gender
role patterns, and expectations.

We all have thoughts about how one should celebrate a birthday, how often a family should vacation at the beach; we have

---

1   Dave Harvey, *When Sinners Say I Do*, 15.

stories packed with ideas for family dinner, family worship, ideas
about how one should school a child and how to fold a fitted
sheet. These stories tucked into our luggage with sin can be very
hurtful in Christian marriage if we are not willing to carefully
unpack our ideals and lay them all out on the master bedroom
floor, alongside our spouse's and sort through the stories and the
sin ever so carefully with the microscope and unraveling tools of
the gospel.

When I was first thinking about marriage to Michael, I would
have told you I had no expectations for marriage except for two
tiny things—I never wanted to have to take out the garbage or
plunge a clogged-up toilet. But what I have learned over time is
the luggage of my life that I brought into my marriage affects my
every day with my husband. In my flesh, with my cozy old woven
threads, I respond to my husband in a way that echoes the story
of my childhood. It is not until I am self-aware of these patterns
that I can gospel-waltz out of them. This again requires the putting off of the old and the retraining of my mind with the renewing of the Holy Spirit through God's Word and prayer. Once I
have put off and renewed my mind, I can then walk in my heavenly
shoes and live out building a new heritage with my husband, a
new heritage that is rooted in the truth of God's redemptive story
and not the stories packed in my luggage of life, luggage that is
threaded through and through with sinful patterns rooted in pride,
self-protection, and a tangled-up identity.

Family Patterns

My father was a guitar player growing up and he plays the guitar
beautifully. Most of the luggage I have unpacked has the beautiful
score of classical guitar music in the background. Every grown-up
should have a release and a disconnect from work and responsi-
bilities; it is healthy to do something for pure pleasure, and for my
father this was guitar playing. This was his hobby and his escape.
There were times in my growing up when I would enter into the
room while he was playing his guitar and want to tell him a story
or ask him a question, but because he was so deep into his talent

and his hobby at times, I wondered if he could hear what I was saying to him.

Unintentionally, I carried this into my marriage. I do not remember ever being upset about my father and his guitar playing. I actually remember this as just being a quirky personality trait about my father and I understood that this disengaging through playing the guitar was simply his escape and release. However, this simple thing, which I never felt hot or cold about in my past, was tucked into the luggage I brought with me into my marriage.

I ended up marrying a guitar player. In our first few months of marriage when I would walk into Michael's office to ask him something, if he happened to be playing the guitar and didn't stop playing or put the guitar away when I began to speak, in a blink of an eye I would go from sweet, loving Rachel to a neurotic basket case, arms and "you don't love me" flying around like gnats in the summertime. When I felt the overreaction, the feelings and words that erupted out of me, I had to go back and carefully unpack my luggage, to see the sin that was entangled around it and unravel it from what was really going on. I had to step out of old patterns and unravel through processing the truth in God's Word. I am seen (Gen. 16:13), my husband loves me, and I need to lay down these past experiences, so I can build a new heritage with him. It is not until my mind is renewed through meditation and prayer that I can walk in the new. The heart work has to be done before I can be ready to fit into the heavenly shoes.

Two Different Shoes

I trained for my first half marathon in 2014. I completed short runs throughout the week, and on Saturday mornings I would meet our church's women's running group for long runs out on the bike trail. One particular morning, we were meeting earlier because of the anticipated heat, and I remember it still being dark as I nursed my baby, brushed my teeth, put on my running clothes, and then quietly crept downstairs to grab some kinesthetic tape for my ankles and my shoes. I was running late and kept the lights off, so I grabbed a left and a right running shoe and drove in my taped and socked feet out to the trail, hoping to just lace up in the parking lot. When I arrived at the trail, I discovered I had a left and a right shoe; however, I had grabbed one old running shoe and one new running shoe. In my persistence I laced up anyway. My goal for the day was eight miles, and since I already had snuck out of my home successfully, I didn't want to waste that time. I thought, *"What harm could I do wearing one old and one new shoe?"*

I was maybe a mile in to my long run when I began to feel the pain in my stride from wearing one old shoe and one new shoe. My left foot began to ache sooner than my right, and as I tried to push through the aches, the aches just began to creep up from my ankles to my shins and to my knees. I knew it wouldn't be long before my hip would begin to twinge, so around the two-and-a-half-mile mark, I decided to turn around and walk back in shame to my car, struggling all the way with negative self-talk and self-contempt. In the moments when I find my performance to be lacking, I am my worst enemy.

As I battled my poisonous self on the long walk back to my car, for two and a half miles I thought about how ridiculous it is to try to run in two different shoes. Not only did my stride look funny, it also felt funny and off-balance.

On my long walk back, I thought about Hebrews 12:1: *Let us throw off everything that hinders and the sin that so easily entangles and let us run with perseverance the race marked out for us* (NIV). If you don't get rid of all of the old . . . you can't run. You can't persevere. I thought about 2 Corinthians 5:17: *If anyone is in Christ he is a new creation. The old has passed away and the new has come.* The old has to go away for you to walk in the new way God is calling you to in the righteousness of Christ.

It seems as silly as my mismatched shoes for me to think about hanging onto my old self as I walk in the new heritage I have in the gospel. Knowing this cognitively is one thing but synthesizing this truth as a pattern of living is much more difficult. I still find myself struggling with my old patterns and my old ways even though I know the gospel. *I still have so much unraveling to do.* There are so many layers beneath the surface, and I feel that daily, as I read

God's Word. God is saying, *"Hey you! Put that off! That is the old way you used to think about that, use My words and walk in them."*

When the old is tangled up in the new, it feels funny. At times in my marriage I have felt the pain of the tension between the old self and the new self. Just like in my two different running shoes—if I try to walk with Christ with some old and some new, after a while this way of off-balanced living will begin to affect me emotionally, spiritually, and physically.

In gospel-centered living, it is necessary to unravel the old, be renewed by the spirit of your mind, and embrace a new pattern, woven in God's Word all the time.

Recently, I have been thinking about an unraveled marriage. What would it look like for me to recognize and put off my old patterns and transform them with the words and power of the gospel? Could I run with more perseverance towards Christ? Could I feel more comfortable and in-step? Would I feel less achy and less off-balance?

I think yes. But I think I still have some unraveling to do as a wife.

When you come into marriage, you bring so many unknown patterns with you—learned patterns from your own family, learned patterns from your friends, learned patterns from your favorite books and movies. Personally, when I find myself hurting, it is my natural tendency to stonewall or shut down, cold shoulder, give a cold but bitter "nothing" when my husband asks me what is wrong. I live with this old, unhealthy pattern tangled up in what I know is true from the Word of God. *If someone sins against you, talk about it* (Matthew 18, summarized and paraphrased). *"Come now, let us reason together," says the LORD. "Though your sins are like scarlet, they shall be as white as snow; though they are red as crimson, they shall be like wool* (Isa. 1:18).

As a wife, I love my husband and I desire to treat him the way God treats him. I don't want to have the old patterns that I have brought from learned ways of the world and have them tangle up the way God has designed marriage in the words from Scripture. Living with the old tangled up in the new looks as silly as those shoes, and it is uncomfortable and unsatisfying. I can't run with the old tangled up in the new in my marriage. I can't persevere to love my husband when my old patterns are tangled up in my new life in Christ.

Unraveling doesn't happen once in a lifetime. Unraveling doesn't happen once a week after a convicting sermon on Sunday morning. Unraveling doesn't even happen once a day. Unraveling happens on the long hard miles of everyday life with your spouse, kids, neighbors, and co-workers. In gospel-centered living, it is necessary to unravel the old, be renewed by the spirit of your mind, and embrace a new pattern, woven in God's Word all the time.

Leaving Expectations and Cleaving to a New Heritage

When I think about the gospel unraveling expectations, when it comes to unpacking the luggage I toted with me into my marriage and the hard work of doing the heart work of putting off, unraveling, and putting on the new self, created after the likeness of God in true righteousness and holiness, I think about the beauty of leaving and cleaving to build a new heritage; and as I leave and cleave, unravel the old to walk in the new, a deeper oneness is created with my husband as I unpack my luggage alongside his to build a new heritage. I am committed to doing the hard work of heart-work because I want to experience what is one of the greatest blessings in gospel-centered marriage, creating a new heritage with my best friend as we walk in parenting and life together, side-by-side as we strive towards honoring the Lord.

> Therefore, shall a man leave his father and mother, and
> shall cleave unto his wife. — GENESIS 2:24a (KJV)

When Genesis was written, it was very common for women to leave their families once they were married. It was actually expected that a woman would leave her family and move into the husband's household, a household which contained multiple generations of wives who left their households to live in a home under the roof and protection of the husband's heritage with his family. At that time, it was implied that the wife would leave her household, but it was actually quite radical for a man to leave his household and cleave to his wife to begin a new heritage. The whole inspired truth from Genesis when we first see the picture of marriage is radical: that man and wife would leave their families, their traditions, and their heritages to cleave to one another.

The word *cleave* here means to become strongly and emotionally attached. And the intentionality of the word "leaving" coming before "cleaving" implies we cannot become strongly and emotionally attached to the new until we leave the old. Once we unpack and leave our old familial heritages, we then can cleave to, or become strongly established in, making a new heritage with our spouses. I want to include here that this is a slow unraveling as I know I have items in my toted luggage that I have yet to unpack, and my husband does as well. But it is a beautiful picture that we are doing the work of unpacking together. We are both taking out the garments, examining them, coming to God's Word and our own personal convictions, and walking in a new heavenly heritage, one that is unique to Michael and Rachel Craddock.

The greatest blessing of marriage is found in the first few pages of Scripture that God calls us to put off old wardrobes and cleave to new ones. This is a beautiful thing because it means new traditions for you, your husband, and your children based on your uniqueness in Christ and the words from Scripture. As husband and wife in a new heritage, you and your husband can decide how you want to honor the Lord when you are building your own heritage. As a married couple, you get to decide together what to do when it comes to family traditions.

God says you shall leave your past and cling to a new present you choose together with your husband. Leaving and cleaving is more than compromising; leaving and cleaving is a melting pot where those old garments are blended together in a cauldron of the gospel to make an entirely new recipe. The traditions your children will look forward to each holiday will be formed as you unravel old expectations, do the hard work of heart work in the gospel, and walk in new heavenly heritages, created after the likeness of God in true righteousness and holiness.

In my new heritage with my husband, I desire to unravel any unintentional expectation I have for him to toss his guitar aside and completely fix his eyes on me as I am speaking to him. I have to fight to unravel that reaction from my heart because this is not a part of the heavenly heritage I want to pass on to my children. This reaction is not rooted in extending mercy and grace; it is rooted in "see me" selfishness. Each time I think to apply mercy and grace to my marriage in this situation, each time I choose heavenly shoes instead of old rotten garments, I get a little bit better at walking in the spirit that is created after the likeness of Christ. With each step I take towards mercy, I develop more of a muscle memory for it. I'm not completely cut and toned in these mercy muscles, but my mercy muscles are in conditioning, and I am thankful just to remember to work them out and walk in them from time to time as I do the heart work to unravel expectations for my husband in marriage.

part five

parenting

parenting and perfectionism

Children, obey your parents in the Lord, for this is right.
"Honor your father and mother" (this is the first
commandment with a promise) "so that it may go well
with you and that you may live long in the land."
Fathers, do not provoke your children to anger, but bring
them up in the discipline and instruction of the Lord.

EPHESIANS 6:1-4

I thought these chapters would be the easiest to write, but instead, they were the most difficult, mostly because all four of my children are under the age of ten, and I am still learning how to synthesize my parenting in the gospel. I have fallen short in many ways, and I am still on the journey of gospel-centered parenting.

Performance Expectations in Parenting

The summer before I had my first child, I was not only visibly pregnant with new life, I was also pregnant with expectation. Neither motherhood nor the idea of it ever came naturally for me. In the same way I never saw myself as a married woman, I never saw myself as a mother either. This was woven in my story of loss. Because I lost my mother at a young age, motherhood seemed distant to me; motherhood seemed foggy when I thought about it—I just couldn't see myself clearly in the role of "mother."

I remember taking my first pregnancy test and almost feeling shock when I saw the positive line on the test strip. Michael was ecstatic, but I was overwhelmed by the unknowns of motherhood and this place which seemed foggy to me. I found myself on the edge of uncertainty, a place where I let fear and my experiences trump my faith in God's provision for me in the unknown. Quickly, I covered up my uncertainty with all the knowledge on being a parent I could muster up. During the summer of my first pregnancy, I read anything I could get my hands on, and with all my head knowledge, my expectations grew and grew for the kind of mother I wanted to be—a perfect one—and the kind of children I would have—perfect ones. In this new season of carrying new life, I found my wandering heart back at my broken cisterns of a performance-based faith.

At the beginning of my motherhood journey I was very much tangled up in fear and the desire to be perfect. I believed with Michael's Master of Divinity and my degree in early childhood education, we would be able to be strong enough parents. I leaned on what we knew: if we read enough and knew enough information, we could check off the boxes and raise smart, well-rounded, athletic, good-looking and kind children. I was pregnant with my first son, but also pregnant with the performance-based expectation of raising up excellent children. That summer I had a big belly and big dreams of bilingual, brilliant, and perfectly obedient children. I once again was at the crossroads of transition, back at my cisterns and clinging to what I knew and how well I could perform instead of depending on the One who knew me. Perfectionism, approval, and a tangled-up view of strength all were deeply woven in my expectations for myself in motherhood.

The First Glimpse of the Wandering Heart of a Child

As a parent, I find myself often frustrated when my children will not listen to me. My expectation for perfection and the reality of my children's imperfections leave me in a hot mess of frustration sometimes. My four children are precious treasures, but my four children have hearts that are prone to wander. No matter how much I prayed for them as infants to never know a day when they were not connected to the personal Savior Jesus, as soon as my children could move about on their own, they pretty much have not listened to a thing I have to say—at first. All of my children are precious and created for glory, but they all have prone-to-wandering hearts, just like their momma.

My first glimpse into the wandering heart of a child was with my firstborn. I'll never forget the fear over faith I had when it came to the electrical outlet in our family room. It was baby-proofed, but I had a big fear that my son would be electrocuted by a baby-proofed outlet in our family room. The knowledge from the baby books pulled on my fear strings instead of my faith strings. I was wacko about this outlet and constantly telling my son not to touch it when he began to crawl around our home.

The outlet was near his toys, and the more I told him not to touch that outlet, the more he desired to touch the outlet. His heart was prone to disregard my words from the very start. He touched the outlet, and I would tell him "no" and remove him from the outlet area. I did this several times to try to communicate consistency. However, when my son began to pull up to stand around eight months of age, I was sitting on the ground playing with him when I watched him crawl over to the outlet, pull up to stand with a sit-to-stand toy, and then reach behind his back to deceitfully touch the forbidden outlet. Behind his back! At just eight months old!

As an educator, I knew this kind of curiosity was developmental, but as a parent, with the tangled-up desire of wanting to have a perfect eight-month-old, this moment really rubbed up against my man-centered expectations. This moment pushed me to a place where I was not in control; I needed to depend on God's consistent work in the heart of my child.

I do not like to be found in places outside of my own control— things I cannot control scare me—but parenting has brought me to a place where I find myself out of control and needing to depend on a supernatural work within the hearts of my children, as well as a supernatural work in my own heart as I learn to trust God as their Story-Weaver and Redeemer.

My second son came just nineteen months after the first, and then my third son, fifteen months after that. I was in my late twenties, I didn't have my mother, and all I wanted was three perfect sons who pooped, slept, and ate on the same schedule. I deeply wanted to control my three sons, so I could fit them into my boxes of perfect parenting. I nursed them, cloth-diapered them, made the organic baby food, disciplined them, taught them to pray, prayed over them, read to them, did early reading flashcards, went to the mommy and me classes, and the baby swimming lessons. I did everything I was supposed to do—except give my sons and myself grace in the imperfect moments. I was so tangled up in do, do (both performance and poop), I didn't have space for grace when I found myself tangled up two-stepping between belief and obedience. I am still recovering from my legalism as a parent, I am still learning how to embrace grace when it comes to this God-given role called motherhood.

And Then . . . God Gave Me Four

I was training for my first half marathon, and we were on a family vacation in Florida. As I went out to run ten miles along A1A near the Atlantic Ocean, the Florida humidity made me feel nauseous. As an Ohioan, I chalked this up to climate change, and my husband picked me up from my run. A day later, my husband watched me devour an entire carton of ice cream by myself, and we both knew something was up—I never eat ice cream. We were pleasantly surprised with my fourth pregnancy. We always dreamed of having four, but never imagined having our four children so close together. When Lydia Jane was born in December, we had four children, four and under.

In those days we memorized the words from Ephesians 6: *Children, obey your parents in the Lord, for this is right.* We sang this verse, read stories about this verse, but constantly I felt like this verse was falling on deaf ears as I experienced imperfections in my children. I frustrated my children with my legalism when we had four children under four. In church I wanted them to be completely still, at school I never wanted a warning mark in their planner. I expected early readers, gifted thinkers, and a little marching tribe of obedient angels. God redeems us from performance-based faith and legalism. He is slowly redeeming me from my tendency to expect perfection from my children. My firstborn has experienced the worst of my performance-based parenting. I have tried in my own effort to churn out perfect covenant children, and at times, I feel I have exasperated my children. There needs to be obedience, but there also needs to be grace.

That first year with four kids four and under, I found myself in a place outside of my control. With my four children, I could no longer check all the boxes, keep the windows and door frames smudge free, or get three children to poop in their diapers all at the same time. When I found myself at the end of my control, I also found the end of my patience. I personally needed grace because I couldn't live up to the expectations I made for myself. I needed grace because I could no longer sustain my children and myself in my performance-based type of mothering. I was exasperated, weary, and at the bottom of another dried-up cistern.

> Children, obey your parents in the Lord, for this is right. "Honor your father and mother" (this is the first commandment with a promise) "so that it may go well with you and that you may live long in the land." Fathers, do not provoke your children to anger, but bring them up in the discipline and instruction of the Lord. — EPHESIANS 6:1-4

Making Room for Grace

The same cisterns I identified as a thirsty way of living when I first heard the gospel as a new Christian in 2004, were popping up in my motherhood in 2014. Just when I thought I had identified, repented of, asked for a change in my inner self, and walked in new obedience in one layer of my life, there was always another layer underneath.

My sin is intimately woven into everything about me. I struggled against the old self as a mom to four children four and under in the same way I struggled against the old self when it came to my view of strength, my identity, and my tangled-up desire to control as a new wife. I still struggle against the old self. Following Jesus in a gospel-centered life is a constant call to unravel our old selves, *daily*. There is always another layer of pride and unbelief underneath the surface. Our hearts are always prone to wander back over to the idols which give us false comfort.

Making space for grace in my life is challenging. I rarely give myself grace. In many ways, I still speak to myself in the same way I did as a fourteen-year-old girl, "Weakness is not an option, you better not cry." My old self is my worst enemy. It is difficult for me to rest in the grace and freedom of Jesus. I cognitively know the gospel, but I struggle to rest in His grace alone. This affects my parenting, because if I cannot extend grace to myself, I am unable to extend grace to others. For me, I have to be intentional about making space for grace, and I need other friends to help me be accountable to the discipline of making space for grace.

My sin is intimately woven into everything about me. I still struggle against the old self. Following Jesus in a gospel-centered life is a constant call to unravel our old selves, daily.

In gospel-centered parenting there is a lot of unraveling going on. There is my personal three-step waltz between repentance, belief, and obedience, my husband's three-step waltz and there are the four (different) individual three-step waltzes of my children. Each of our waltzes follows the same pattern of repentance, belief, and obedience, but each of our waltzes is different because each of us is woven together uniquely. We are a bunch of sinners waltzing in the same house and bumping into one another as we unravel along the way.

Most of my overreactions to the behaviors of my children (or just my frustration of not being able to use mind control on them) are from the unhealthy woven threads of pride or unbelief in my own heart. These overreactions come when I find myself at the end of my time, my patience, my emotional ability, and my mental ability. Parents will always, as limited human beings, be brought to the end of themselves in the now and the not-yet of this life. In human strength alone, Christian parents are not enough. But in Jesus, when parents are at the end of themselves, God makes those found in Christ to be enough by His grace and His mercy. In gospel-centered parenting, making space for grace is necessary. In Christ there is never-ending mercy, patience, self-control, and kindness. You will never reach the end of it. This is hard work. This is seeing our sin as big, and God's grace and mercy as bigger, and then transferring that same principle onto our children as we model gospel-centered living in our interactions with them.

I confess, when I was a new parent wrapped up in control, perfectionism, and human strength, I could not see the beauty of this gospel-centered way of parenting. I had to come to the end of myself, where the well of my human patience, perfectionism, and desire to control ran dry. I had to bump up against the wall of frustration many times while I was tangled up in legalism. Having four children in four years was the shattering of my dried-up cisterns of pride, perfectionism, control and bootstrap-pulling. When I couldn't sustain myself any longer, I needed the spring of living water to sustain me in the trenches of parenting in the now and the not-yet. I needed a God whose mercy was new every morning for me and my children. I needed to make space for grace.

The steadfast love of the Lord never ceases;
his mercies never come to an end; they are new
every morning; great is your faithfulness.

LAMENTATIONS 3:22-23

chapter twelve

the gospel unravels the american dream of parenting

Love the Lord your God with all your heart and
with all your soul and with all your strength.
These commandments that I give you today are to be
on your hearts. Impress them on your children. Talk about
them when you sit at home and when you walk along
the road, when you lie down and when you get up.

DEUTERONOMY 6:5-7 (NIV)

The Gospel Unravels Performance-Based Parenting

Having walked almost a decade in parenting, what I know now
is that parenting has so little to do with what kind of person you
are, what degrees you have, or how many parenting books you've
studied. In gospel-centered living, parenting must revolve around
the gospel with repentance, belief and obedience—and be covered
in prayer. If we believe in the gospel, as parents, we have to look
deeper than behavior modification and what our children look like
outwardly. As parents, we have to be very careful not to two-step
with our children between legalism, moralism, or antinomianism;
all three will leave us tangled up, frustrated, and unable to get

beneath the surface-level behaviors with our children.

As parents we must teach our children repentance, belief, and obedience in a circular motion. In the gospel, as explained in the earlier chapters in Ephesians, we believe it is God who changes the heart of a child and gives children eternal hope. Our children were created for glory by a very good Creator. They are saved by God's grace and mercy, not based on their performance. Our children need the eyes of their hearts to be enlightened, so they can fight sin at its deeply woven threads of pride and unbelief. Transformation is spiritual for our children, in the same way it is spiritual for adults, and transformation is a slow unraveling.

In gospel-centered living, parenting must revolve around the gospel with repentance, belief and obedience—and be covered in prayer.

Being alongside your children in gospel-centered parenting is a life-on-life journey. Life-on-life journeys are messy and life-on-life journeys are intimate. It's messy because it is hard work to fight through surface-level behaviors to get to the heart of your child. It is intimate because getting to the heart of a child takes time and requires a personal and unique relationship. Gospel-centered parenting must be covered in prayer. As parents we must constantly be praying God will transform the hearts of our children and to continue to transform our own hearts as parents as we walk in the nitty-gritty of raising up sinners in the now and the not-yet.

> Just as a nursing mother cares for her children, so we
> cared for you. Because we loved you so much, we were

delighted to share with you not only the gospel of God but our lives as well. — 1 THESSALONIANS 2:7b-8 (NIV)

Unraveling the American Dream

My American Dream of raising smart, well-rounded, athletic, good-looking, and kind children was unraveled in the gospel. It wasn't until I understood the truth, that my first priority as a parent is to raise my children to know the gospel, that my previous ideals about parenting and raising good American citizens could unravel away. I had to be renewed in the spirit of my mind. I said I didn't believe in showing my kids a performance-based gospel, I said I wanted to get to their hearts, but boy! did I overreact when my children were not behaving perfectly.

Directly after the words in Deuteronomy 6:5, the Greatest Commandment, *You shall love the Lord your God with all your heart and with all your soul and with all your might,* the same words which first penetrated my heart that I was missing the mark of living a perfect life before a Holy God, are the words of how to pass on the Good News Story of Jesus to the next generation: *You shall teach them diligently to your children, and talk of them when you sit in your house, and when you walk by the way, and when you lie down and when you rise* (Deut. 6:7 ESV). These words have changed the way I think about raising my children. My first priority on the other side of the cross as a redeemed believer in Jesus is to teach my four children to love God, love others, and be known in community with Christians: to know God, make God known, and be known. I desire for my children to have transformed hearts instead of well-trained heads. I believe the fruits of a transformed heart will one day, by God's mercy, produce gospel-woven citizens.

Woven in the gospel of Jesus in the now and the not-yet of this life, "we are more sinful and flawed than we can believe but at the same time more loved and accepted than we can dare to hope." [1] In parenting, my idea of the American Dream for my children is unraveled away. In the unraveling, I can give my children a gospel-

---

1   Keller, *The Meaning of Marriage: Facing the Complexities of Commitment with the Wisdom of God,* 46.

centered assurance of love and hope that permeates through being accepted at the lunch table or loved by peers. A transformed heart deeply woven in the gospel will help my children navigate all of life. This transformed heart will produce love, joy, peace, patience, kindness, goodness, faithfulness, gentleness, and self-control through the Holy Spirit.

In the gospel, the desire for performance-based parenting is challenged by God's Word. Oh! How my heart wanders to performance too often! I feel the tension between the gospel and being performance-based when I find myself stuck in the ultimate joy-sucker: comparison. When I am concerned about performance, I find myself always watching how well my children are measuring up to everyone else—comparing, competing, perfecting, achieving. This keeps me focused on people and keeps my eyes away from Jesus.

In the gospel, we can teach our children to see beyond the comparisons and pressures of this life and teach them to look to the One who does the perfecting. It is quite upside-down and inside-out for me to look past behavior and fight to get to the hearts of my children. It is quite radical as someone who has so many years of drinking from stagnant cisterns of muddy water laden with achievement, approval, accolades, self-perseverance, and The American Dream. It is an unraveling of the old patterns and what I thought I knew about raising children and being renewed in the spirit of my mind to say, "Jesus, make my focus in parenting not be on outward behaviors, but on the heart."

> The LORD does not look at the things people look at. People look at the outward appearance, but the LORD looks at the heart. — 1 SAMUEL 16:7b (NIV)

Parenting in the Front Row

I preach the gospel to myself every Sunday in the front row at church while my husband preaches from the pulpit, a gospel that is centered around Jesus, and not focused on others or their approval of my children and how I parent them. Some would say two is company and three is a crowd . . . I am going to infer here

134

that four children in the front row may be considered a circus, especially in a one-parent-to-four-kids ratio.

One Easter Sunday, one of my husband's first as lead pastor of our church, the room was full, the white lilies were beautiful, the trumpet played as the congregation sang "Christ the Lord Is Risen Today." My children were dressed in their most beautiful, spring church outfits. My boys were in matching pastel chinos, white shirts, bow ties, and suspenders, my daughter in a smocked dress and large bow. As I gazed down the row, taking in the beautiful sight of my children, the beautiful sounds of the alleluias, the beauty of Christ rising from the grave, I saw one of my sons remove a large booger from his nose and then . . . eat it—in the front row at church, on the day we celebrated the Resurrected Jesus!

My first priority as a redeemed believer in Jesus is to teach my four children to love God, love others, and be known in community with Christians: to know God, make God known, and be known.

In my personal shame and humiliation, I had to take a step back out of my pride, my heart of perfectionism which all too easily gets caught up in appearances, and I had to remember the Lord is concerned about the condition of my heart and the heart of my child, more than the salty snack my child chose during worship. I desire to see my children this way, to see them as God sees them. I desire for my children to be who they are fully in the front row at church and know, no matter what, booger-eating and all, they are deeply loved by the Resurrected Savior.

135

When I unravel my ideal of well-behaved kids in the gospel, my heart is not troubled when I see my children stumble, get warning marks in their planners, or eat boogers in the front row at church. I can pray for more peace, more patience, and more self-control. I can remember that my children are sinners in the now and the not-yet just like I am. This gospel-centered freedom moves me away from the unrealistic expectation that my children will be perfect on this side of the new heavens and the new earth. This gives me peace.

> Peace I leave with you; my peace I give you. I do not give to you as the world gives. Do not let your hearts be troubled and do not be afraid.. — JOHN 14:27 (NIV)

My Imperfect Children

In my parenting, I have struggled to desire perfection from my children, but time and time again I find myself frustrated because my children are sinners. My children stumble. I have experienced their wandering hearts, even as elementary and preschool students. The gospel moves me to breathe deeply on the journey of childhood imperfections.

In parenting, unraveled from my tangled-up desire to perfect and my tangled-up longing for The American Dream, I see my four stumbling children as God sees them: precious, uniquely knit together and wonderfully made (Ps. 139:13-14). In their stumbling, it is not easy to see them this way; in the trenches when I receive calls from their teachers or experience their stumbling at home, my flesh first wants to respond like a crazy person. You may know someone like her: crazy eyes, snarled lip, raised voice, arm movements, stomping heavily up the stairs. However, I have gospel renewal in my mind through the Spirit. Once I experience this renewal through prayer, I can be moved to compassion for my children. Only in the compassion of the Lord can I correct stumbling children outside of anger and impatience. In the gospel I can remember that God is in the difficult waters with them too. I don't need to over-control or be the one throwing out life

136

preservers when my children stumble. God is in the difficult waters of stumbles and trials with my children, too. God promises the waves of difficulty will not overcome either of us. *When you pass through the waters, I will be with you; and when you pass through the rivers, they will not sweep over you* (Isa. 43:2a NIV).

When I parent out of my own knowledge and strength, I miss showing my children dependence on an active God. I miss showing them the gospel. My entire paradigm for raising up children is unraveled and turned upside down in Jesus. Every cistern I found myself drinking from back when I first believed—approval, acceptance, pride, achievement, The American Dream, and all these standards for worldly living—is not as deeply satisfying as drinking from the spring of Living Water when I find myself parenting through difficult seasons. Focusing on the One who pursued my heart when I wasn't even asking for a transformed life helps me unravel the desires of my flesh to control and over-protect the precious lives of my children. My children are precious to God, and I believe God is pursuing them in the difficult waters too.

In the gospel, I can demonstrate repentance and freedom in imperfections as I turn away from the cisterns of comparing my children to others or loving them based on how well they make me look on a Sunday morning. In the gospel, I can unravel the tangled-up desire of The American Dream for my children and feel free from the yoke of slavery of having the very best children. God is able to do immeasurably more than all I can ask or think in the life of my children. *For it is by grace you have been saved, through faith—and this is not from yourselves, it is the gift of God—not by works, so that no one can boast* (Eph. 2:8-9 NIV).

In unraveled parenting, I pray to the One who pursues hearts and I work to cultivate the hearts of my children to be aware of the cisterns they are prone to wander back to and lead them to dependence on the spring of Living Water. In the gospel I need this for my own life and for the lives of my children. I desire for us to have a heavenly address at the feet of Jesus before I desire a big house and a perfect family on the street of The American Dream.

part six

grief

chapter thirteen

threads of unhealthy grief

Finally, be strong in the Lord and in his mighty power.
Put on the full armor of God, so that you can take
your stand against the devil's schemes.

EPHESIANS 6:10-11

Miscarriage and the Resurfacing of Unhealed Grief

I was twenty-six years old in a banquet room celebrating the marriage of two new friends. Michael and I had been serving at North Cincinnati Community Church for six months at this time. I was slicing the wedding cake for the guests of the bride and groom, placing the small slices of cake on the plates before me. My husband and nine-month-old son were among the crowd beyond the table. I was about eight weeks pregnant. I felt excited, scared, and overwhelmed about adding another baby to our family. The baby I was carrying and my son in the crowd beyond the table would only be fifteen months apart.

As I sliced the pieces of cake and placed them on plates, suddenly I could feel emotionally in my heart and physically in my body, something was not right. I realized I was miscarrying my baby while I was slicing and serving wedding cake in a banquet hall. I panicked. I was in a room filled with people, but immediately I felt alone. This loss of my child was pulling on my threads of unhealed grief.

I could not rush to the privacy of the public restroom stall quickly enough. I could not sprint, although I wanted to; I feared making a scene at my new friend's wedding. Once I entered the hallway, I could not even find where the restroom was located. On the outside, I asked strangers politely where to find the restroom behind a false smile, but inwardly I was chaotic.

The immediate heartbreak of loss settled in when I found the privacy of a public restroom stall. In my pain, I reverted to my shame-space; my inner monologue once again chanted ugliness in this moment of pain. In my heartbreak, when I was all alone, I listened to the "what is wrong with me" lies and the "I did something wrong" anthems that seep in so easily when I find myself back in a shame-space. I took a great beating from Satan's lies and sticky shame while I was alone in the restroom stall. *I didn't eat well enough, I lifted something too heavy, my heart rate was too high at my last workout.* The scroll of every single thing I could have done wrong rolled out before me. As I listened to all of my shortcomings, I failed to make space for faith or grace.

Blame and shame both worked together to bring me down into the trenches of faithless despair. I felt the shame—that there was something wrong with me. In the restroom stall, after blame and shame had given me a good beating, I led myself to believe I was incredibly alone and I was the only one to ever miscarry a child. I led myself back to the place of loss and uncertainty, with the tangled-up belief that no one else in this world could bear this burden with me.

When my husband came to me with our nine-month-old son, I was already thoroughly ashamed of what I felt like I had done. In the few moments in the restroom stall, I had rebuilt walls of self-protection around my heart. I couldn't even let my husband come to me in my pain. I sat in the car next to him on the long drive back from the wedding. Physically we were inches apart, but emotionally I was light years away. My old self took over in my shame and prevented intimacy between my husband and me in that moment of loss and suffering.

At twenty-six years old, in trenches of despair, the unhealed places in my heart reminded me that in my life, people die. In my despair, I clung to my learned behaviors of both apathy and cynicism. In the car, I didn't even know how to cry. I just stared coldly out the window, the same way I did when my father told me my mother was going to pass away. While we drove, my thought life was untamed and free to continue the severe beating it had started hours before in the restroom stall.

When I found myself at the doctor's office in an ultrasound room, my doctor confirmed, the baby I once carried no longer had a heartbeat. My husband was visibly upset. By this time, I was emotionally comatose. The pain and loss of my miscarriage felt very real, but the pain and hurt of my previous loss and learned behaviors enabled me to be numb to the pain. I reverted to my old patterns of shutting down and retreating to a cave of isolation.

In the months that followed, I never really scratched at the surface of this pain. I pulled up my bootstraps and carried on, looking for silver linings but always wondering about the child I had lost while I was slicing and serving wedding cake. Even in a room full of people, I felt alone in this part of my story. When grief is tangled up in shame, grief is isolating. Grief can make one feel like a square peg in a round-hole type of place. In the isolation of a shame-space is a breeding ground for the wounds of loss to become lies.

I am almost a decade from this moment, and my heart hurts to think about that time. What hurts is not the loss, as much as it is the lies that crept in and defined me in my suffering; even when I knew Christ as a personal Savior, I stumbled back into a shame-space. When grief is tangled up in old unhealthy patterns, it gives Satan a loud voice. This voice seems louder than truth, especially when the shame keeps you in hiding and away from gospel-centered community.

What I know now is that when grief comes, you have to battle the lies with truth. *Finally, be strong in the Lord and in his mighty power. Put on the full armor of God, so that you can take your stand against the devil's schemes* (Eph. 6:10-11 NIV). This battling requires the putting on of truth, so you can fight against the lies Satan whispers to you when you find yourself standing in a shame-space. It is when we feel alone that Satan and the lies we believe breed and grow. There

143

are three things I have learned to help me when I am feeling stuck in the lies I believe: I invite people into my pain—no matter how alone I feel; I recognize the unhealthy threads in my unique story; and I use scripture to replace the lies with truth from God's Word, because God is a God who is near to those who are suffering.

1. You are not alone in your grief. Fight to invite others into your pain.

When grief is tangled up with shame, Satan will lead you to believe you are alone. With shame in the forefront, truths become distant whispers. Satan wants us to feel disconnected from the ones who breathe life back into our souls. In loneliness and isolation, Satan's power over patterns of self-destruction are at work; this is where lies are loud and clear, and the hope of the gospel is hard to hold onto.

Statistically, one in four women will experience pregnancy and infant loss in some form or another. The more I stepped out of my dark restroom stall of shame and entered into conversations with my husband and with other women who had walked through pregnancy and infant loss as well, the more I was able to identify the threads of pain in this story. I was not able to heal from my pain after my two miscarriages (I walked through another miscarriage between our third and fourth children) until I could identify the threads which were causing pain in the first place.

> But when anything is exposed by the light, it becomes visible. — EPHESIANS 5:13

When I kept my suffering in the darkness, I blamed myself for that baby being lost behind that table. I carried the weight of that burden for so long. For weeks, months, and even years I let my mind wonder: What if I had not eaten that slice of deli meat, or what if I had not forgotten my vitamin that day? What if I had been sitting instead of standing? All these things were too much for my heart to bear alone. Satan's subtle "what ifs" kept the blame finger pointed in my direction. The darkness within me needed to be exposed to the light.

I needed others to speak truth to me when truth was a faint whisper behind the loud clamoring of my own patterns of self-destruction. I needed others to remind me, the loss of this baby was not because of anything I did or did not do. When I was the girl behind the table slicing and serving wedding cake, I needed the courage to step out of the restroom stall, where I took a harsh blame and shame beating, and into the arms of others alongside me.

God is always present with us in sufferings, and He gives us the people of His church to help strengthen us when we can't hold ourselves up any longer.

Although I felt alone, I was never alone at all. God is always present with us in sufferings, and He gives us the people of His church to help strengthen us when we can't hold ourselves up any longer. One of my favorite Old Testament passages is when Joshua is battling the Amalekites in Exodus 17. When Moses holds up his hands, Joshua receives favor from the Lord and advances in the battle. Over time, Moses becomes weary—physically, mentally, and emotionally weary from holding up his hands. He alternates from hand to hand, but he comes to a place where he cannot hold up his hands on his own any longer. When Moses is at the end of his own physical, emotional, and mental strength, God provides others to come alongside him.

> Whenever Moses held up his hand, Israel prevailed,
> and whenever he lowered his hand, Amalek prevailed.
> But Moses' hands grew weary, so they took a stone and

> put it under him, and he sat on it, while Aaron and Hur
> held up his hands, one on one side, and the other on
> the other side. So his hands were steady until the going
> down of the sun. And Joshua overwhelmed Amalek
> and his people with the sword. — EXODUS 17:11-13

Who is at your sides to hold your arms up when you cannot hold them up any longer? Who has God put alongside you to help you remember we are never alone in our sufferings? The lies of Satan can only be squashed when darkness is brought to light within gospel-centered community. Satan has no power in the light of the gospel.

2. Your story is unique. Your personal story and self-awareness are important to help you identify the lies you believe.

Just because other women have experienced pregnancy and infant loss does not mean you are merely a statistic. Your story is unique. Your baby was unique. Your pain and your grief journey will be unique. Other women may have shared a similar experience, but other women and their experiences, cannot remedy your unique pain. Other women can simply sit in the darkness of pregnancy and infant loss alongside you, while you wait to walk through the stages of grief in God's healing timetable made uniquely for you.

It is normal to experience shock, denial, anger, and sadness in the wake of pregnancy and infant loss. It is emotionally healthy to let yourself grieve. Vulnerability is strength. Tears are strength. Holding fast to the hope of the cross is strength, especially when the answers to the why and what if questions of life seem to go unanswered.

3. God knows suffering and understands the pain of loss. Find scriptures to help you cling to truth in your personal grief.

When the truth of the gospel is no longer a faint whisper, I can remember I know a God who knows suffering and loss. I know a God who sent His own Son to die on the cross. I know a God who experienced separation from His own Son.

This is where true healing is found, by stepping out of the darkness and drawing near to the One who knows suffering. Healing will not come at the snap of a finger, nor at the pulling up of a bootstrap; this healing will be a slow unraveling of unbelief as you draw near to God in prayer and read His promises in His Word, in the community of others. This unraveling is messy, jagged, and unorganized. This is the kind of healing that comes from brokenness, where there are no clean and clear answers, but simply open and needy hands.

> The Lord is near to the brokenhearted. — PSALM 34:18a

> Blessed are those who mourn for they shall be comforted. — MATTHEW 5:4

> He will wipe every tear from their eyes, and death shall be no more, neither shall there be mourning, nor crying, nor pain anymore, for the former things have passed away. — REVELATION 21:4

> Trust in the Lord with all your heart and do not lean on your own understanding. — PROVERBS 3:5

> Come to me all who are weary and heavy laden, and I will give you rest. . . for I am gentle and humble in heart and you will find rest for your souls.
> — MATTHEW 11:28-30 (NASB)

Vulnerability and stepping out of the darkness is a sliver of my pregnancy and infant loss story. There are pieces here I still have yet to unravel as I walk in this life, but I truly believe there are deep healing powers in the gift of opening up the chapters of our lives and letting others truly see us. There is healing power as we share our stories, and healing power as we listen to the unique stories of others. The more we open ourselves up and let ourselves be seen, the more we realize we are never alone.

chapter fourteen

the gospel unravels grief

Therefore, take up the whole armor of God,
that you may be able to withstand in the evil day,
and having done all, to stand firm. Stand therefore,
having fastened on the belt of truth, and having put on the
breastplate of righteousness, and, as shoes for your feet,
having put on the readiness given by the gospel of peace.
In all circumstances take up the shield of faith,
with which you can extinguish all the flaming darts of
the evil one; and take the helmet of salvation, and
the sword of the Spirit, which is the word of God, praying
at all times in the Spirit, with all prayer and supplication.

EPHESIANS 6:13-18a

God Unravels Us from the Threads of Unhealthy Grief

It was summer time, but the air was surprisingly cool and sweet. As I ran on the trail along the Little Miami River, my thoughts turned to my mother. That day would have been her sixtieth birthday. Eighteen and a half years after that dark, gray day on Sycamore Creek Drive, eighteen and a half years lived without her and only fourteen lived with her. In this season of running, my headphones were quiet, and I only could hear the sounds of my stride, the river, the birds, and the occasional rustling of a deer coming out of the woods to drink from the stream. The sun speckled through the canopy of the trees above me and exposed the spider webs laced with morning dew.

That year I was on a journey of running a full marathon in memory of my mother. When I began, I had asked God to change me. When I asked for this change, I was desiring for God to strengthen me. I wanted to be strong and run with perseverance in the same way my mother boldly faced breast cancer during the days of my childhood. Woven in a tangled-up view of strength, I desired to push myself to complete a full marathon, something I knew would be a personal challenge. When I first asked for this change, I was asking God for a quick, strength power-up. Easily, I forgot that when we ask for God to change us that change never happens comfortably like we imagine. I imagined a gentle candlelit fire lighting up inside my heart, a gentle call to strength that would make me rise, ready to fight, ready to conquer the journey in my own might.

My worldly view of strength was still tangled up in my grief, and I forgot that when we are strengthened through exercise there is heavy lifting and our muscles become sore and tender. It is in the tenderness and soreness that muscle fibers go through their cellular process to fuse together and form new muscle protein strands. Muscle strength and growth occur when the new strands of muscle protein synthesis are greater than the muscle protein breakdown.

In my months of training on the trail, I waited on the gentle flame to ignite me, but instead, I learned that my refinement in strength had to come through a tender and sore heart. My grief and strength threads woven in pain and the old self needed to be unraveled and broken down. The synthesis and a new understanding of constructing grief through new threads connected to Christ needed to be woven at a greater rate than the old threads were unraveling away.

At times when I ran in that season, it felt like my very own heart was being ripped out. On the trail beneath the canopy of trees, I felt an unraveling of what I thought I knew about grief for the first time. I once believed if I could check the boxes in the stages of grief, it would all come to an end. In the transforming power of the gospel, I know these old ideals must be unraveled away. The process of unraveling grief has been a process of unlearning old patterns through tears, tenderness, and vulnerability. Once the old patterns are unraveled away, there is space for the synthesis of new healthy threads to form and grow in the redemptive tapestry God is writing for me, woven in grace and truth. This new thread synthesis is woven in who God is and embracing the characteristics of being His daughter instead of old patterns woven in what I think I should do or who others say I am. It is only through the breakdown of the old patterns and the synthesis of what God is teaching me about who I am, who He is, and what He defines as strength that I remember the process to a renewed heart is the opposite of a gentle, cozy flame.

Just when I thought I could outrun my tender places by training for a full marathon, I felt God calling me back to them, to face them, to put off the old, to be transformed and walk in the new. I had to continuously undress and redress, to put off what felt natural to me for so many years and put on the new clean wardrobes, in true righteousness and holiness made after the likeness of God. *Assuming that you heard about him and were taught in him, as the truth is in Jesus, to put off your old self, which belongs to your former manner of life and is corrupt through deceitful desires, and to be renewed in the spirit of your minds, and to put on the new self, created after the likeness of God in true righteousness and holiness* (Eph. 4:21-24).

God wants to do the unraveling for me, and all I have to do is lie down on the grass and let Him do it. The unraveling I do in my own strength is only surface deep, but God is calling me to a deeper unraveling. God really wants to change me from the inside out, the same way Aslan wanted to transform Eustace, a rotten boy, and release him from the captivity of his dragon skins.

> The very first tear he made was so deep that I thought
> it had gone right into my heart. And when he began

pulling the skin off, it hurt worse than anything I've ever felt. The only thing that made me able to bear it was just the pleasure of feeling the stuff peel off. Well, he peeled the beastly stuff right off—just as I thought I'd done it myself the other three times, only they hadn't hurt—and there it was lying on the grass: only ever so much thicker, and darker, and more knobbly-looking than the others had been. And there was I as smooth and soft as a peeled switch and smaller than I had been. Then he caught hold of me—I didn't like that much for I was very tender underneath now that I'd no skin on—and threw me into the water. It smarted like anything but only for a moment. After that it became perfectly delicious and as soon as I started swimming and splashing I found that all the pain had gone from my arm. And then I saw why. I'd turned into a boy again. . .

After a bit the lion took me out and dressed me . . . in new clothes.

— **C.S Lewis**, *Voyage of the Dawn Treader* [1]

As I ran on the trail in memory of my mother, I felt as if God was tearing deep down to my heart to bring change from the inside out. As He unraveled the old idea of hiding behind layers of a firm fortress, I felt freedom from the firm fortress and I embraced the freedom to feel angry with my grief. In the unraveling, I had to wrestle with my pain and look at it in the face with anger, hot tears, questions and the untying of my bootstraps. In the wrestling, my marching boots were removed and left out on the trail. In the wrestling beneath that canopy and speckled fragments of sunshine, I felt the tenderness and the soreness of my heart transforming and the callouses on my heart softening. Beneath that canopy I began to feel, for the first time, fully healed through letting go and allowing myself to feel the pain.

I saw the girl I once was at the beginning of this mission, without a clue of how to live out a life in the front row in church,

---

1   C.S. Lewis, *Voyage of the Dawn Treader,* 109.

still clinging to and drinking from the cistern of performance and how well she could perform this role of pastor's wife to a watching world. On the trail along the Little Miami River, I recalled Lewis and Clark on their own mission traveling three thousand miles during a long harsh winter. I thought about who I had been as a new wife ten years before and the miles God had had me traveling across during my own "three thousand miles of harsh winters," the threads from all my winding up tight and unbelief in my own heart. In all of these seasons of unraveling I have seen that strength, identity, perfectionism, marriage, parenting—all seem to be tied to those graying moments on Sycamore Creek Drive. They seem to bring me back with pain I have buried deep beneath my own knobbly dragon skins. On the trail I felt God giving me an opportunity to feel everything I had once thought I was not allowed to feel. For once I felt permission to look my grief in the face, to wrestle, to find closure, to feel broken, human, undone, and to find the peace of God which transcends understanding. Strength didn't come like a gently lit candle, but instead, as a scorching, torch-like, refining flame.

I allowed myself to feel hate as I ran. I hated cancer as I ran. My heart ached and burned. I cried about how the last time I remember speaking to my mother was probably over some kind of fight we were having while I was an emotional fourteen-year-old. I hated myself as I ran for being such a difficult raging teenager as my mother was breathing her last breaths. The hate and anger I felt made my heart ache and burn. I saw this teenage version of myself, and in my anger, I felt freedom to let her go and forgive her. I saw my seasons of total darkness and I could forgive myself for them. On the other side of forgiveness, I could finally embrace my delivery from total darkness and allow my feet to reside on the streets of the kingdom of His Beloved Son with whom He is well pleased.

Underneath that canopy with the asphalt trail beneath my feet, I asked God why I had to live through having four kids in four years without a parent to call, without someone to listen, without extra hands and without an unconditional group of people-whom-you-call-about-things-you-can't-tell-anyone-else village. I cried about my kids not having Grandma Shelley. I cried because she missed knowing them, she missed knowing my husband. I saw my expectations of what I thought it would have looked like to be a parent with my own mother on the other end of the phone. I wrestled with the truth, in the now and the not-yet. This story of my mother and me was not the way it's supposed to be, and I left the expectation of the way I wished my story had been written on the trail alongside my bootstraps.

On a tiny bike trail along a tiny river I cried tears of fullness. My winding up tight unraveled behind me, my past self, like a shadow, no longer loomed behind me but completely unraveled away through facing my demons, letting them go and forgiving myself as God has forgiven me.

I no longer allow the identity-defining words of "the girl from total darkness" linger behind me, nor do I feel like a robotic pastor's wife wearing a mask to appear strong, performing, prepared and properly casseroled. I feel fullness with the long thread of my past unraveled from me. I trust in a God who is unraveling every layer of protection I have placed around my heart. And beneath all that winding up tight, I have seen glimpses of the girl God created me to be once again. She has been there all along, I can never outrun her; I simply need to forgive her and see her with the redemptive eyes of the gospel.

> Blessed be the God and Father of our Lord Jesus Christ, who has blessed us in Christ with every spiritual blessing in the heavenly places, even as he chose us in him before the foundation of the world, that we should be holy and blameless before him.
> — EPHESIANS 1:3-4

Shalom-Peace

Along those miles on the trail, I looked my grief in the face. You can walk with God for over a decade, having lost someone two decades before, having read good books on grief, and still fail to look grief in the face. I never had looked my own grief in the face before. I had never taken the time to be mad and sad, frustrated, or disappointed. I had never given myself permission to be vulnerable. Grief brings nasty feelings, and for so long I just wanted to push them down rather than feel them. Pulling up my bootstraps and burying my hurts was so much easier than learning about this tender place hidden deeply beneath all my winding up tight. I had put band-aids on gunshot wounds, and for so long I had let myself walk in a false sense of peace, not woven in anything except what I thought it looked like to be strong and carry on.

This false sense of peace was a breeding ground for insecurity, false hope, cynicism and a whole lot of feeling sorry for myself. But in taking hold of my grief, learning how and where I am tender, unraveling the old strings, I found the comfort of a God who knows suffering.

> He heals the brokenhearted and binds up their
> wounds. — PSALM 147:3

On the other side of the refinement and finding strength through vulnerability, I have somehow found thankfulness to see past the hurts and see how much God has provided for me along the "three thousand miles of journeying across the harsh winters" of my own heart.

I found thankfulness because I was an outsider, "the girl from total darkness," who was brought in and transferred into the kingdom not because of anything I did, but because God chose me in Him before the foundation of the world. Now I have the right and privilege as a resident of this heavenly kingdom to His new mercies every single morning, new mercies which are laden with shalom-peace.

Shalom-peace is peace, harmony, wholeness, completeness, and tranquility. This feeling of shalom-peace is an inner manifestation of the gospel through a transformed heart. Shalom-peace is not swayed by circumstances, anxieties, shame, fear or sufferings. Shalom-peace is looking forward to the eternal hope that God is making all things new, things in heaven and things on earth (Rev. 21:4). When Jesus saw His disciples the night before His crucifixion, He left the disciples with this message of shalom-peace.

Jesus knew what was to come for Him, but in His circumstances, He preached shalom-peace. *Peace I leave with you; my peace I give to you; not as the world gives do I give to you. Let not your heart be troubled, nor let it be fearful* (John 14:27 NASB). Shalom-peace transcends the pangs of pain, the schemes of Satan, and the rule of shame in the now and the not-yet of this life. In shalom-peace we know this world is not the way it is supposed to be, but we look forward to eternal hope and glory, where God will make all things new and there will be no more crying and no more tears.

> He will wipe away every tear from their eyes, and death shall be no more, neither shall there be mourning, nor crying, nor pain anymore, for the former things have passed away. — REVELATION 21:4

In this thankfulness of shalom-peace, after the wrestling and the unraveling of all the hiding behind the threads I once committed to winding up tight, I felt whole. On the other side of the hard journey of looking grief in the face, I found genuine thankfulness, wholeness, peace and tranquility, not the false sense of peace that brushes over fears and hurts like a well-intended greeting card, but the kind of thankfulness which is the fruit of a changed heart. The mission I have been traveling on has not been cozy or comfortable or easy like I first expected when I began in St. Louis or even back in that passenger seat on Sycamore Creek Drive, but as I look around me, I have realized that I can choose to see big hurts, feel sorry for myself, and make the emptiness big, or I can choose to see a big God, who knows big hurts, who is walking with me in sorrow, and I can be thankful for the places where He has me now.

Asking God to change me from the inside out has been a scary thing, but when I felt human and desperate enough, when I was so tired of trying to heal myself in my thirsty ways of living, I began to trust something divine, to let God do the work in my heart. When He began pulling the knobbly skins off, it hurt worse than anything I'd ever felt, but I promise what came after the hurt was something delicious; it was the freedom to let the old unravel away.

. . . according to the riches of his glory he may grant
you to be strengthened with power through his Spirit
in your inner being, so that Christ may dwell in your
hearts through faith—that you, being rooted and
grounded in love, may have strength to comprehend
with all the saints what is the breadth and length and
height and depth, and to know the love of Christ
that surpasses knowledge, that you may be filled with
all the fullness of God. — EPHESIANS 3:16-19

Shalom-Peace and a New Society

God wants to do the renewing for us. In this pleasure found in the
unraveling of the old there is freedom from hiding pain and the
tangled-up desire of having to walk in the role of perfectly being
a pastor's wife, church member, or parent. The expectations of
perfectionism unravel away in shalom-peace. There is no longer
a yoke of slavery to thirsty living, drinking from the broken cisterns
of pleasing others through appearing to live out God-given roles
with perfectionism. In the unraveling, we can see clearly the
unique men and women God has woven us together to be and
free ourselves from the yoke of slavery of seeing people and
circumstances big and God small.

In shalom-peace we see a God who is the author of every
story. Before the fullness of time, He knew exactly what He was
up to when He delivered those who were far off and those who
were near—from total darkness—and placed them in the new
society of the church. This new society is filled with others who
are wrestling in seasons of pride, unbelief, and shame. Before the
fullness of time, God has been writing a redemption story for the
whole world, to unite all things to Himself in Jesus.

There is harmony in the new society, the Church, and completeness in Christ, and tranquility in the uniquely knit-together
men and women God is making us all to be. *I . . . urge you to walk
in a manner worthy of the calling to which you have been called, with all
humility and gentleness, with patience, bearing with one another in love,*

157

eager to maintain the unity of the Spirit in the bond of peace (Eph. 4:1-3). Within shalom-peace society within the church, we are responsible to gospel-waltz—to put off the old, be transformed, and walk in the new heavenly shoes we've been given in Christ's work on the cross. The old is gone and the new has come in the mercies which are lavished upon us every morning. In the synthesis of a transformed heart, we can live in community and apply this transforming shalom-peace to other struggling sinners in the church. With hearts transformed by shalom-peace, we can see others in their heavenly shoes too, and we can learn to waltz well alongside them.

With hearts transformed by shalom-peace, we can see others in their heavenly shoes too, and we can learn to waltz well alongside them.

Shalom Over Shame

For the first time in as long as I can remember, even through the unraveling and the knowledge of my brokenness in the front row, I feel wholeness—wholeness because I fix my eyes on the hope of one day being complete and lacking nothing. I know I am from total darkness, but at the Day of Christ, I will reside on the streets of the new heavens and the new earth. The inner manifestation of shalom-peace is greater than the power of the shame from my past. God takes unlikely people and transfers them to His kingdom to the praise of His glory. This humbles me, encourages me to embrace my brokenness, and burdens me to pass this story of unraveling on to you with hope that you may one day be unraveled and find shalom-peace and wholeness in an active God who is redeeming people and reconciling the whole world to Himself. I hope that you too may reside on the streets of the new heavens and the new earth, not because of who you are, where you are from or what you have done, but simply because you trust in God and what He has done. Wherever you come from, or however you have wound-up your threads, my hope is that you would simply lie down on the grass and let God unravel every piece of unbelief from your heart so you can see yourself as God sees you too: precious in His sight, clothed after the image of God in true righteousness and holiness. I am right there learning to trust God and continuing to unravel alongside you.

It would be nice and fairly nearly true, to say that
"from that time forth, Eustace was a different boy."
To be strictly accurate, he began to be a different boy.
He had relapses. There were still many days
when he could be very tiresome. But most of those
I shall not notice. The cure had begun.

C.S Lewis, *The Voyage of The Dawn Treader* [2]

---

2   Lewis, *The Voyage of The Dawn Treader*, 112.

part seven

a redemptive tapestry

chapter fifteen

God unravels the old to reveal a redemptive tapestry

So we do not lose heart. Though our outer self is
wasting away, our inner self is being renewed day by day.
For this light momentary affliction is preparing for us
an eternal weight of glory beyond all comparison,
as we look not to the things that are seen but to the things
that are unseen. For the things that are seen are transient,
but the things that are unseen are eternal.

2 CORINTHIANS 4:16-18

In the now and the not-yet it is quite easy to lose heart. We are all human and we are all finite. Many of us feel the ripple effects of sin, shame, and death in this world. Our outer selves waste away in seasons of injury, childbirth, aging, sickness, addiction, anxiety, and depression. Our momentary afflictions weigh down our hearts when we feel so overcome with our grief and the brokenness we experience in life on earth. Sin, shame, and death are like a mucky water that makes gospel-truth difficult to see. We all can identify with the truth that this world is just not the way it was supposed to be, but God doesn't leave us to live here on earth in the darkness of the mucky water. God gives us His Son Jesus to help us see through the mucky water. Jesus is the light that enables us to hold onto shalom-peace in a world that is just not the way it is supposed to be.

> Therefore, having this ministry by the mercy of God, we do not lose heart . . . For God, who said, "Let light shine out of darkness," has shone in our hearts to give the light of the knowledge of the glory of God in the face of Jesus Christ.
>
> But we have this treasure in jars of clay, to show that the surpassing power belongs to God and not to us. We are afflicted in every way, but not crushed; perplexed, but not driven to despair; persecuted, but not forsaken; struck down, but not destroyed; always carrying in the body the death of Jesus, so that the life of Jesus may also be manifested in our bodies. For we who live are always being given over to death for Jesus' sake, so that the life of Jesus also may be manifested in our mortal flesh. So then, death is at work in us, but life in you. — 2 CORINTHIANS 4:1, 6-12

In the middle of the publication of this book I went through the process of my annual check-ups with my doctors. Because of the medical history of my family, I like to make sure I am staying on top of things regarding my health, so I can be intentional about being around for my four children for as long as I possibly can. I have known for a few years that I carry the PALB2 gene mutation which elevates my risk for breast cancer by sixty percent. When I first learned I carry the gene mutation, I was told I would not be a candidate for a double mastectomy and reconstruction. I was told to undergo imaging every six months to watch for early signs of breast cancer.

However, over time the recommendation for women who carry the PALB2 gene mutation has changed, and just when I thought I was almost finished writing this book, I was given the medical recommendation to undergo a double mastectomy and reconstruction. Initially the shock and the grief both my husband and

I felt upon hearing this news left us trekking through the ripple effects of mucky water in the now and the not-yet. Our momentary affliction weighed us down. Our mucky circumstance and our grief dimmed the light of the gospel, and shalom-peace felt like a slippery, mucky mess we couldn't hold on to.

> . . . when I fall, I shall rise; when I sit in darkness, the Lord will be a light to me. — MICAH 7:8

It took me a few weeks to recognize this momentary affliction as a chapter in the greater redemptive story God is weaving for me. It took intentionally abiding in God through His Word and His people to hold on to shalom-peace when it felt slippery and to see the light through the muck when the light seemed to be dimmed by darkness. God is using this physical change in my body to continue to unravel the old and weave a redemptive tapestry. In the small death of a double mastectomy, I will experience a newfound freedom. I will be loosened from living with the fear of developing breast cancer in the same way my mother did. I will be freed from the fear of my children having to walk through the pain of losing a parent at a young age. Through loss I will be redeemed from this hard place in my story. It is painful to unravel and die, but in the unraveling God is making a beautiful, redemptive tapestry.

I have this treasure, the light of Jesus, in a jar of clay. My jar of clay has been quite marred and broken. My life has been broken, crushed, and unraveled, but my hope is not in the transient and marred things that I can see around me; my hope is in the beautiful eternal tapestry that God is weaving in and through me as I die to myself and live to shine the light of the One who died for me and conquered death so I could live. The old is passing away, and new life really does happen in the redemption of Christ's death on the cross. He raises me through tiny deaths every day. His light shines through the broken, crushed, and unraveled places in my tapestry. My momentary afflictions are transient, but who God is making me to be through new life in Christ is eternal. This new redemptive tapestry is the woman God is unraveling me to be.

Since we have the same spirit of faith according to what has been written, "I believed, and so I spoke," we also believe, and so we also speak, knowing that he who raised the Lord Jesus will raise us also with Jesus and bring us with you into his presence. For it is all for your sake, so that as grace extends to more and more people it may increase thanksgiving, to the glory of God. — 2 CORINTHIANS 4:13-15

My main motivation to write all of these things down and bind them in a book is so you may know that there is light and beauty underneath what can feel like darkness and chaos. God is making a redemptive tapestry for me and for you in the unraveling. I hope that through this marred, fractured, unraveled jar of clay others will see Jesus shine through the broken places. I hope this grace extends and unravels the hearts and stories of those who read it, so we all may increase in thanksgiving to the glory of God.

I have told you these things, so that in me
you may have peace. In this world you will have trouble.
But take heart! I have overcome the world.

JOHN 16:33 (NIV)

acknowledgments

First, I would like to thank my husband, Michael, for encouraging me to keep writing, even when I was not the very best writer. After all, I only applied to colleges that did not require admissions essays—writing was a gift I didn't even know I had. Michael has been faithful to love and support me in all my unraveling, and I am grateful to have him alongside me on this journey.

I would also like to thank my children: Ezra, Asher, Caleb, and Lydia Jane—four gifts that I truly don't deserve. The four of them help me see just a glimpse of how much God loves His children and teach me how I need to unravel on a daily basis. It is a joy to be their mother.

I need to thank the fifty plus people that helped me write this book. I cannot name all of them, but my writing is a community project. Many men and women read, edited, revised, encouraged, and prayed over this project. I am so grateful to each of you for donating your time, your gifts, and your wisdom to *Slowly Unraveled*, especially to CDM Publishing and the team that has believed in this project and seen what it could become.

I am grateful to the ministry of Campus Outreach. In 2003, a small staff team moved to my college campus at Eastern Kentucky University to pioneer a new ministry in the state of Kentucky. God used the men and women on that team to show me what it means to love others well—and how to love God's Word. Through the ministry of Campus Outreach, my life was forever changed. I am so grateful God has woven this ministry into the patchwork of my story.

I would like to thank Parakaleo. In 2012, I attended my first Basic Intensive Retreat with Parakaleo and digested every word of *Beyond Duct Tape*. God used Parakaleo to help me embrace my unique identity in Christ and unravel the expectations I had for myself as a pastor's wife. Parakaleo is a ministry that comes alongside church-planting wives—they make the gospel practical, memorable, and life-giving.

The ministry of Perimeter's Life on Life Missional Discipleship is dear to me. I first was able to understand the gospel in a practical way through reading Randy Pope's Life Issues books as a senior in college. I am in my fifth year of leading a Life on Life Group with the women at North Cincinnati Community Church, and I enjoy how the material weaves God's Word, the gospel, and personal story together; as well as encourages men and women to share their stories with others. This book is filled with truth I learned while sitting around a table with my Life on Life group.

I am grateful for the staff, the session, and the men, women, and children at North Cincinnati Community Church. You all have given me grace and shown me love as I have slowly unraveled and learned what it looked like for me to be a pastor's wife, while I sat in the front row at our church.

For my family, and the community that has watched me struggle after the death of my mother—I have so many dear friends who have stuck beside me during the hard times and the triumphant times. It is a gift to have men and women in my life who have loved me in the dark seasons and the light seasons.

And thanks be to God. The author of the best stories. He is good, and He is making all things new.

story workbook

and

discussion guide

Chapter 1: Personal Story Work

Chart the major events of your life by using the grid below. On the left, write the major events in chronological order and write about why this was a major event in your life, what emotions come to mind when you think of each event. When you peer back into these moments, do you feel joy, sorrow, pain, wholeness? On the right, use a +/- symbol to indicate how this drew you into a relationship with God (+) or caused your distance from Him (-).

My Story:

Life Event	How This Impacted My Faith
My mom dies when I am 14. I completely lose identity and significance. I begin to fill my life up with many temporary things: cutting, drinking, drugs, being promiscuous. I feel like an outsider in every group I am in because I am hiding my pain behind many layers of masks.	−
I go to college and church, I begin to fill my life up with good works to amend for the dark season I experienced in high school.	−
Someone reads the book of John with me and shares their testimony with me. I am challenged by God's Word.	+
I get involved in Bible study.	+
I meet Michael and we get engaged. He says he wants to go to seminary.	+/−
We move to St. Louis and Michael starts seminary. This is a new unknown season and I revert to my known shame-behaviors.My head and my heart are not in the same place.	−
The girl from total darkness	−
Ezra is born, we move to Cincinnati, Michael begins working as a youth pastor.	+
Living in Cincinnati and identity.	+
We have four kids in four years and I am given way more than I can handle.	+
Michael's pastoral candidate process.	+
I finally spend time grieving the death of my mother and unraveling the lies from my past.	+
Now, I still am able to identify the lies that Satan uses to make me feel shame, fear, and doubt.	+

Your Story:

Life Event	How This Impacted My Faith

Use this space to pick three life events and write about how each of these events have affected the way you experience God, yourself, and others.

Life Event 1	Life Event 2	Life Event 3
How did this affect the way I saw God?		
How did this affect the way I viewed myself?		
How did this affect how I interacted with others?		

Chapter 1: Questions for Personal Reflection or Small Group Discussion

1. Open your Bible to Ephesians 1. Write down the words that jump out to you about God the Father and about Jesus.

God	Jesus

2. Read Genesis 1 and 2. What do you notice about God and His relationship with Adam and Eve?

3. Read Genesis 3:7-10. Mark the places where you find elements of shame in this passage. Write below how we experience these same elements of shame in the present time.

> *Then the eyes of both were opened, and they knew that they were naked. And they sewed fig leaves together and made themselves loin-cloths. And they heard the sound of the Lord God walking in the garden in the cool of the day, and the man and his wife hid themselves from the presence of the Lord God among the trees of the garden. But the Lord God called to the man and said to him, "Where are you?" And he said, "I heard the sound of you in the garden, and I was afraid, because I was naked, and I hid myself"* (Gen. 3:7-10).

2. Look further in Genesis 3. How does God provide for Adam and Eve in their shame and hiding, and what does this have to do with shame in the present day?

3. Describe the difference between guilt and shame. Use the definitions in the chapter to help you come up with a definition for guilt and shame in your own words.

4. How do you think about personal brokenness? How do you define strength? What do you think about weakness?

5. How do your definitions above help you or hinder you from reaching out towards those who are walking in shame and personal brokenness? How does Genesis 3:21 help you think about the way God reaches out to those hiding in a shame-space?

Chapter 2: Personal Story Work

Think about one of the earliest times of trial in your personal story. What did you feel during this season in your life? Did you feel shame during this time? Write about the wounds or the lies you believed during this season.

Life Event	Wounds
Lies	**Vows**

Chapter 2: Questions for Personal Reflection or Small Group Discussion

1. Read and mark Ephesians 1:3-10. List all of the things from Ephesians 1 that God gives to believers in Jesus. How can shame distort this truth?

> *Blessed be the God and Father of our Lord Jesus Christ, who has blessed us in Christ with every spiritual blessing in the heavenly places, even as he chose us in him before the foundation of the world, that we should be holy and blameless before him. In love he predestined us for adoption to himself as sons through Jesus Christ, according to the purpose of his will, to the praise of his glorious grace, with which he has blessed us in the Beloved. In him we have redemption through his blood, the forgiveness of our trespasses, according to the riches of his grace, which he lavished upon us, in all wisdom and insight making known to us the mystery of his will, according to his purpose, which he set forth in Christ as a plan for the fullness of time, to unite all things in him, things in heaven and things on earth* (Eph. 1: 3-10).

2. Read and mark Ephesians 2: 8-9. What does this have to do with performance? How does shame and unworthiness distort this truth? How can shame lead us back into a cave of isolation?

> *For by grace you have been saved through faith. And this is not your own doing; it is the gift of God, not a result of works, so that no one may boast* (Eph. 2:8-9).

3. What is harmful about seeing 2 Timothy 2:3 through a lens tangled up in legalism?

> *Share in suffering as a good soldier of Christ Jesus* (2 Tim. 2:3).

4. Why do you need to three-step in a circular motion around repentance, belief and obedience?

5. How would you gently encourage a believer who is easily forgetting what is hers in Jesus?

Chapter 3: Story Work

Write about a time when you felt tension between the old patterns and new patterns in your life. Are you actively identifying patterns of the sinful nature in your life? What truths unravel the places where your heart is prone to wander?

Fill in the t-chart to show battles of your old self against the Spirit of God in your heart.

Old Self (The Flesh)	New Self (Spirit-Filled Living)

Chapter 3: Questions for Personal Reflection or Small Group Discussion

1. Read and mark Ephesians 1:17-19a. What is Paul's prayer for the Ephesians? Why is this important for believers?

> *I keep asking that the God of our Lord Jesus Christ, the glorious Father, may give you the Spirit of wisdom and revelation, so that you may know him better. I pray that the eyes of your heart may be enlightened in order that you may know the hope to which he has called you, the riches of his glorious inheritance in his holy people, and his incomparably great power for us who believe* (Eph. 1:17-19a NIV).

2. Read and mark Galatians 5:1. Think and write about areas in your life where you may be submitting to a yoke of slavery rather than to God's call to freedom in the gospel.

> *It is for freedom that Christ has set us free. Stand firm, then, and do not let yourselves be burdened again by a yoke of slavery* (Gal. 5:1 NIV).

3. We live in the now and the not-yet here on this side of heaven. We know of the hope that is to come, yet we struggle with the effects of sin in this life. Write out some ways you experience the tension between the pain of the now and the hope of the not-yet in your own life.

4. Read and mark Galatians 5:16-17. What are two possible forms of pride found in battling the old self? Identify the times when you battled each of the two forms of pride.

But I say, walk by the spirit and you will not gratify the desires of the flesh. For the desires of the flesh are against the desires of the Spirit and the desires of the Spirit are against the desires of the flesh. For these are opposed to one another, keeping you from doing the things you want to do (Gal. 5:16-17).

5. Read and mark 2 Corinthians 12:9-10. How are the eyes of your heart enlightened by the words of this verse? How does having the eyes of your heart enlightened by this verse enable you to embrace the community of believers in the church?

> "My grace is sufficient for you, for my power is made perfect in weakness." Therefore, I will boast all the more gladly of my weaknesses, so that the power of Christ may rest upon me. For the sake of Christ, then, I am content with weaknesses, insults, hardships, persecutions, and calamities. For when I am weak, then I am strong (2 Cor. 12:9-10).

6. Define the gospel in your own words.

Chapter 4: Story Work

Continue to fill in your Story Work Chart. This time add a lie you may have believed during each significant life event.

Life Event	+/−	The lie I believed during this time

Chapter 4: Questions for Personal Reflection or Small Group Discussion

1. Read and mark Ephesians 2:1-10. Identify the words pertaining to one's life before Christ and one's life after Christ. Use the table below to help you compare and contrast.

> *And you were dead in the trespasses and sins in which you once walked, following the course of this world, following the prince of the power of the air, the spirit that is now at work in the sons of disobedience— among whom we all once lived in the passions of our flesh, carrying out the desires of the body and the mind, and were by nature children of wrath, like the rest of mankind. But God, being rich in mercy, because of the great love with which he loved us, even when we were dead in our trespasses, made us alive together with Christ—by grace you have been saved—and raised us up with him and seated us with him in the heavenly places in Christ Jesus, so that in the coming ages he might show the immeasurable riches of his grace in kindness toward us in Christ Jesus. For by grace you have been saved through faith. And this is not your own doing; it is the gift of God, not a result of works, so that no one may boast. For we are his workmanship, created in Christ Jesus for good works, which God prepared beforehand, that we should walk in them* (Eph. 2:1-10).

Life Before Believing in Christ	Life After Believing in Christ

2. From Ephesians 2:1-10: How does one achieve royal status? Describe what we do in contrast to all of the things God does.

3. Read and mark Genesis 1:27 and Psalm 139:13-14. How did God create you? How does this help you see yourself in God's greater redemptive story?

> *So God created man in his own image, in the image of God he created him; male and female he created them* (Gen. 1:27).

> *For you formed my inward parts; you knitted me together in my mother's womb. I praise you, for I am fearfully and wonderfully made. Wonderful are your works; my soul knows it very well* (Ps. 139:13-14).

4. Read and mark Jeremiah 2:13. How do you see your heart as an idol factory? What idols are there that may lead you into the "if I could just then I could" problem? How is this a thirsty way of living? Identify some of the idols of your heart below.

> *My people have committed two sins: They have forsaken me, the spring of living water, and have dug their own cisterns, broken cisterns that cannot hold water.* (Jer. 2:13 NIV).

5. How do the wounds, lies and vows you identified in the story work section distort the way you see your identity in Christ?

Chapter 5: Story Work

Recall names you were called from your past during the significant seasons in your story. How were these names "sticky" to you? Describe how these names may distort the way you see your identity in Christ?

Life Event	Shame-Name	How has this shame-name impacted your identity?

Chapter 5: Questions for Personal Reflection or Small Group Discussion

1. Read and mark Ephesians 2:17-22. What kind of people groups are listed in this passage of Scripture?

> *And he came and preached peace to you who were far off and peace to those who were near. For through him we both have access in one Spirit to the Father. So then you are no longer strangers and aliens, but you are fellow citizens with the saints and members of the household of God, built on the foundation of the apostles and prophets, Christ Jesus himself being the cornerstone in whom the whole structure, being joined together, grows into a holy temple in the Lord. In him you also are being built together into a dwelling place for God by the Spirit* (Eph. 2:17-22).

2. From Ephesians 2:17-22. What is the purpose of all of these people coming together? How is this community in contrast to communities in the world? See also 1 Peter 2:4-12.

3. Write about a time when you walked in fear over faith. How does fear hinder your relationship with others in the body of Christ as well as your relationship with God?

4. Read and mark Colossians 1:13-14. Illustrate this beautiful gospel picture using pictures and words. How does this align with the words in Ephesians 2:17-22?

> *He has delivered us from the domain of darkness and transferred us to the kingdom of his beloved Son in whom we have redemption, the forgiveness of sins* (Col. 1:13-14).

5. Everyone has felt seasons of isolation within the church. What gospel truths remind you that you are no longer a stranger or an alien, but now a fellow citizen? How does this help you see yourself within gospel-community in the church?

Chapter 6: Story Work

Unravel the wounds, lies and vows of your past.

1. Find 2-3 verses from Scripture you can use in battle against this sticky part of your old self and write them below. 2) Write a prayer of repentance for the tangled-up view of your identity based on a wound, lie or vow. 3) Write a prayer of supplication asking God to help you believe this truth and change you from the inside out. 4) Then replace the lie by memorizing one of the verses you chose from Scripture in Step 1.

My story:

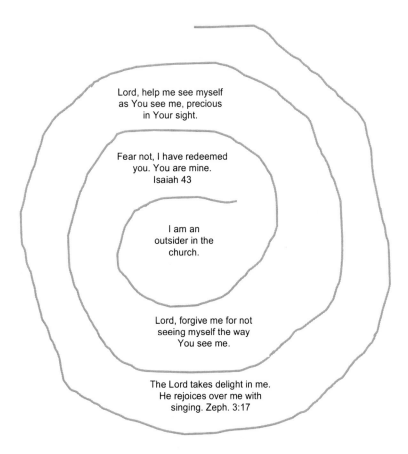

Lord, help me see myself
as You see me, precious
in Your sight.

Fear not, I have redeemed
you. You are mine.
Isaiah 43

I am an
outsider in the
church.

Lord, forgive me for not
seeing myself the way
You see me.

The Lord takes delight in me.
He rejoices over me with
singing. Zeph. 3:17

Your Story:

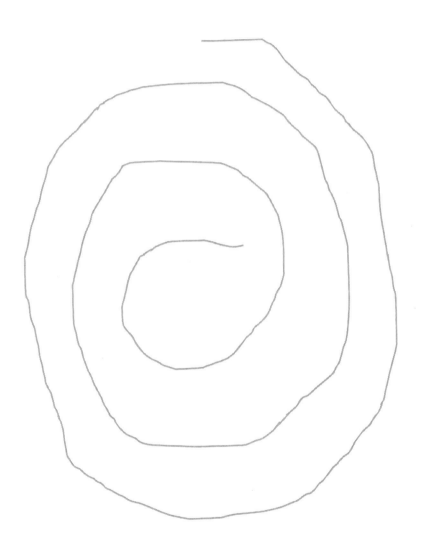

Chapter 6: Questions for Personal Reflection or Small Group Discussion

1. Read and mark Ephesians 3:6, 14–19. What is Paul's main hope for the Ephesians in this passage of Scripture? Why is this so important?

> *[Those who were far off] are fellow heirs, members of the same body, and partakers of the promise in Christ Jesus through the gospel . . . For this reason I bow my knees before the Father, from whom every family in heaven and on earth is named, that according to the riches of his glory he may grant you to be strengthened with power through his Spirit in your inner being, so that Christ may dwell in your hearts through faith—that you, being rooted and grounded in love, may have strength to comprehend with all the saints what is the breadth and length and height and depth, and to know the love of Christ that surpasses knowledge, that you may be filled with all the fullness of God* (Eph. 3:6, 14–19).

2. List the three steps in the "Gospel Waltz." Identify where you two-step when it comes to your identity. Why are all three steps important for gospel-centered transformation?

1.	What does this look like in my life?
2.	What does this look like in my life?
3.	What does this look like in my life?

What does it look like in your life to get tangled up in two-stepping?

3. Read and mark 2 Corinthians 5:17. Do you think it is possible to just put off the old and put on the new without waiting on spiritual transformation? Explain.

If anyone is in Christ, he is a new creation, the old has passed away; behold, the new has come (2 Cor. 5:17).

197

3. Take your favorite verse and walk through each level in Bloom's Taxonomy of Learning with the verse. What would be different about your life at each level of learning with your favorite verse?

Remembering:	
Understanding:	
Applying:	
Analyzing:	
Evaluating:	
Synthesizing:	

4. How can we be better encouragers to men and women in our churches when it comes to Christian identity?

Chapter 7: Story Work

Can you remember a time when you felt under the yoke of slavery to perfectionism? Was it over entertaining someone in your home, having the "right" answers in Bible Study, or simply walking away from a conversation and perfecting it on your drive home? Write it down. How does the yoke of slavery to perfectionism impact your personal story? What verses can you use to help you unravel from slavery to perfectionism?

Times I have seen slavery to perfectionism pop up in my life:

How this impacts how I see myself and community with others:

Verses I will use to intentionally help me walk in new trust and obedience:

Chapter 7: Questions for Personal Reflection or Small Group Discussion

1. Read and mark Ephesians 4:1-7. What are the things listed in this passage that help those within the church embrace unity with one another?

> *I therefore, a prisoner for the Lord, urge you to walk in a manner worthy of the calling to which you have been called, with all humility and gentleness, with patience, bearing with one another in love, eager to maintain the unity of the Spirit in the bond of peace. There is one body and one Spirit—just as you were called to the one hope that belongs to your call—one Lord, one faith, one baptism, one God and Father of all, who is over all and through all and in all. But grace was given to each one of us according to the measure of Christ's gift (Eph. 4:1-7).*

2. Why is it important to apply these truths to yourself before you can live in unity with others?

3. Read and mark Romans 12:4-8. How does perfectionism prevent us from living according to the measure of Christ's gift as mentioned in Ephesians 4:7? What does this have to do with identity in Christ?

> *For as in one body we have many members and the members do not all have the same function, so we, though many, are one body in Christ, and individually members one of another. Having gifts that differ according to the grace given to us, let us use them: if prophecy, in proportion to our faith; if service, in our serving; the one who teaches, in his teaching; the one who exhorts, in his exhortation; the one who contributes, in generosity; the one who leads with zeal; the one who does acts of mercy, with cheerfulness* (Rom. 12:4-8).

4. Identify a time when you were disappointed over a moment of imperfection. How did this keep you from being in vulnerable community with others?

5. Read and mark Galatians 5:1 Write about the beauty of the gospel freeing us from slavery to perfectionism.

> *It is for freedom that Christ has set us free. Stand firm, then, and do not let yourselves be burdened again by a yoke of slavery* (Gal. 5:1 NIV).

Chapter 8: Story Work

Write about a time when you felt free to show up with empty hands. What was it about the situation that helped you feel free to have empty hands? How can you extend that feeling to others in your life?

Take the "Are You a Slave to Perfectionism" Quiz from Chapter 8.

Questions to assess how perfectionism may impact your personal life:

- *Do you find yourself saying yes to too many things?*

- *Do you have higher expectations for yourself than you do for others?*

- *Are you easily frustrated when things do not go the way you expected them to go?*

- *Is there a critical voice in your consciousness which feels louder at times when you stumble?*

- *Do you leave a conversation and then are occupied by things you should have said?*

- *Does this rehearsal of the conversation keep you preoccupied in your thoughts?*

These questions will help you assess if perfectionism is preventing you from vulnerable community with others:

- *Do you find the critical voice in your head speaking when you notice imperfection in others?*

- *Are you quick to point out and correct the imperfections in the lives of those around you?*

- *Do you fail to see others as in process in the gospel?*

- *Do other people know the real you or just the perfected parts of you?*

- *Do you care how others see you more than you care about your position in Christ?*

- *Does your need to do things right keep you from stepping out in the community of faith within the church?*

- *Do you assume others have high expectations for you? your parenting? your Sunday School answers?*

- *Are you reluctant to jump into community in the church because you fear you are not enough or not ready?*

Take one of the questions you answered "yes" to above and gospel-waltz through this area of perfectionism using the chart on the following page.

Area to repent of:	Scripture I need to pray to believe in my heart:	How I will be intentional about walking in new obedience/ How others can help me to walk in new obedience:

Chapter 8: Questions for Personal Reflection or Small Group Discussion

1. Read and mark Ephesians 5:8-10. List patterns of living where you find yourself still walking in old patterns.

> *For you were once darkness, but now you are light in the Lord. Live as children of light (for the fruit of light is found in all that is good and right and true) and try to discern what is pleasing to the Lord* (Eph. 5:8-10 NIV).

2. How does community call us out of our old patterns? Read and mark James 5:16.

> *Therefore, confess your sins to one another and pray for one another, that you may be healed. The prayer of a righteous person has great power as it is working* (James 5:16).

3. Read and mark 1 John 4:18. How does perfectionism connect with fear? How does the slavery to fear prevent us from loving ourselves and others well?

> *There is no fear in love, but perfect love casts out fear. For fear has to do with punishment, and whoever fears has not been perfected in love* (1 John 4:18).

4. Read Proverbs 4:23. Discuss a time when you found yourself aware of the tangled-up desires of your heart and how those tangled-up desires prevented you from vulnerable Christian community.

> *Above all else, guard your heart, for everything you do flows from it* (Prov. 4:23 NIV).

5. List the people in your life who you feel are people who pursue your heart when you are retreating back into a shame-space. How do they effectively pursue you? Who are those you see when they are retreating back into caves of isolation? How do you pursue others to live a life of freedom in the gospel?

Chapter 9: Story Work

How does your natural way of communicating and resolving conflict impact your story? What are the unhealthy threads you see in the way you talk with others or process conflict? Is the way you communicate with others rooted in the way you have always communicated, or do you see God transforming your communication and conflict resolution by the application of His Word? Explain.

How my conflict was handled in my family upbringing:

How this impacts the way I engage conflict in the present day:

Verses that will help me fight to communicate with others in a way that glorifies the Lord:

Chapter 9: Questions for Personal Reflection or Small Group Discussion

1. Read and mark Ephesians 5:22-24. According to Scripture, how should wives relate to their husbands in marriage? How does sin tangle up this command in God's Word? Read also Genesis 3:16. Why is it unnatural for a person to submit to the authority of another person? Apply how submission to another has shown your reverence for Christ. Describe the types of relationship to which this command would not apply.

> *Wives, submit to your own husbands, as to the Lord. For the husband is the head of the wife even as Christ is the head of the church, his body, and is himself its Savior. Now as the church submits to Christ, so also wives should submit in everything to their husbands* (Eph. 5:22-24).

> *To the woman he said, "I will surely multiply your pain in childbearing; in pain you shall bring forth children. Your desire shall be contrary to your husband, but he shall rule over you"* (Gen. 3:16).

2. Read and mark Ephesians 5:25-30. What is the command for husbands in this passage of Scripture? List all the ways husbands are to love their wives.

> *Husbands, love your wives, as Christ loved the church and gave himself up for her, that he might sanctify her, having cleansed her by the washing of water with the word, so that he might present the church to himself in splendor, without spot or wrinkle or any such thing, that she might be holy and without blemish. In the same way husbands should love their wives as their own bodies. He who loves his wife loves himself. For no one ever hated his own flesh, but nourishes and cherishes it, just as Christ does the church, because we are members of his body* (Eph. 5:25-30).

3. Read Philippians 2:1-5. How does this relate to the gospel and marriage? How does this help you think differently about submission?

> *So if there is any encouragement in Christ, any comfort from love, any participation in the Spirit, any affection and sympathy, complete my joy by being of the same mind, having the same love, being in full accord and of one mind. Do nothing from selfish ambition or conceit, but in humility count others more significant than yourselves. Let each of you look not only to his own interests, but also to the interests of others. Have this mind among yourselves, which is yours in Christ Jesus* (Phil. 2:1-5).

4. How would you like your marriage to be a picture of the gospel to outsiders? If you are not married, when have you seen a picture of the gospel in marriages of those around you?

5. Why is it necessary to live in unity with our spouses in gospel-centered cultures in our homes? How do gospel-centered marriages strengthen the church?

Chapter 10: Story Work

Write about your family patterns. Write about how you have celebrated birthdays, holidays, gone on vacations, addressed gender roles, and about the parenting styles of your parents and you (if you have children). How do these family patterns impact the expectations you have for people around you?

Important family traditions from my upbringing:

Important gender roles I saw lived out in the lives of the family members who raised me:

How do these things impact my life today? What are some traditions or roles I am going to be intentional about leaving so I can cleave to a new heritage?

Chapter 10: Questions for Personal Reflection or Small Group Discussion

1. Read and mark Ephesians 5:31-33. Summarize what Paul is saying to the church in Ephesus in these verses.

> *"Therefore a man shall leave his father and mother and hold fast to his wife, and the two shall become one flesh." This mystery is profound, and I am saying that it refers to Christ and the church. However, let each one of you love his wife as himself, and let the wife see that she respects her husband* (Eph. 5:31-33).

2. From Ephesians 5:31-33: List all the things you should leave from your past before you can cleave to your spouse in marriage.

3. Read and mark Hebrews 12:1-2 and summarize this passage. What does perseverance in marriage have to do with leaving and cleaving?

> *Therefore, since we are surrounded by so great a cloud of witnesses, let us also lay aside every weight, and sin which clings so closely, and let us run with endurance the race that is set before us, looking to Jesus, the founder and perfecter of our faith, who for the joy that was set before him endured the cross, despising the shame, and is seated at the right hand of the throne of God* (Heb. 12:1-2).

4. Write out Genesis 2:24. Why was this command radical for the culture of Israel? Why is it radical for us now in the present time? Describe a culture of leaving and cleaving. Explain the challenges of leaving and cleaving in your own life.

5. What elements of old behavior do you have tangled up in the new life you are called to in the gospel? How does this prevent you from freedom within gospel-centered community (in marriage or with others)?

Chapter 11: Story Work

Look back at the significant events in your life from your story chart in Chapter One. Identify how well you made space for grace for yourself during these significant seasons.

Life Event	Was there evidence of space for grace during this time? What did that look like?

Chapter 11: Questions for Personal Reflection or Small Group Discussion

1. Read and mark Ephesians 6:1-4. What are the ways we are to care for our children (or those we influence) in gospel-centered parenting (or community)?

> *Children, obey your parents in the Lord, for this is right. "Honor your father and mother" (this is the first commandment with a promise), "that it may go well with you and that you may live long in the land." Fathers, do not provoke your children to anger, but bring them up in the discipline and instruction of the Lord* (Eph. 6:1-4).

2. How can our sin distort this gospel-centered way of parenting?

3. Write about a time when you had unrealistic expectations for your children or write about what expectations you would have for yourself as a parent. Discern whether or not these parenting expectations are derived from the Word of God or the world surrounding you.

4. Write how you intentionally practice giving grace to yourself and others the same way God has lavished His grace upon you.

5. Read and mark Lamentations 3:22-23. What does this mean for you as you unravel? How does this impact your being alongside others and your children as they unravel? Compare and contrast the times you have bumped into others graciously with the times you have bumped into others ungraciously.

> *The steadfast love of the Lord never ceases; his mercies never come to an end; they are new every morning; great is your faithfulness* (Lam. 3:22-23).

Chapter 12: Story Work

Using the chart that follows, write the major events of your life in the left column. Based on the work you have been doing in this story workbook, in the right column find passages from Scripture to go with each major life event. These verses could be those that sustained you during a difficult time or truths that you were not applying in your pride and unbelief. Try to find scripture for each major event. How is God unraveling your story?

My Story:

Life Event	A lie I believed at this time	Truth that sustained me at this time	Scriptures I am finding to shed gospel-perspective on this season
My mom dies when I am 14. I completely lose identity and significance. I begin to fill my life up with many temporary things: cutting, drinking, drugs, being promiscuous. I feel like an outsider in every group I am in because I am hiding my pain behind many layers of masks.	I am alone. I am not enough. I am not right. I am an outsider. I need to be stronger. I have to appear perfect. If I can control my world and what others see, I won't hurt again.	Not a believer, I do not know truth, but I do feel broken.	Ephesians 1: 3-10
I go to college and church, I begin to fill my life up with good works to amend for the dark season I experienced in high school.	I need to perform to earn love. If I do well and perform well, I will be loved and happy. God will save me if I become good in my own strength.	Not a believer, I do not know truth, but I feel like I need something to connect me to God.	Jeremiah 2:13
Someone reads the book of John with me and shares their testimony with me. I am challenged by God's Word.	I was not good enough for church.	I didn't have to be good enough for church.	Ephesians 2:8-9
I get involved in Bible study.	Performance is tangled up a little bit in my life as a new Christian. I wanted to perform Christianity well.	Your word is a lamp to my feet and a light to my path.	Matthew 5:6

I meet Michael and we get engaged. He says he wants to go to seminary.	Outsider feelings resurface.	Let us keep our eyes fixed on Jesus the author and perfecter of our faith.	Hebrews 12
We move to St. Louis and Michael starts seminary. This is a new unknown season, and I revert to my known shame-behaviors. My head and my heart are not in the same place.	Outsider feelings, performance-based mentality. John Stott says, "How quickly we forget what is ours when we become followers of Jesus."	Share in suffering like a good solider of Jesus Christ.	I can do all things through Christ who strengthens me.
The girl from total darkness	Shame. Not good enough.	Colossians 1:13-14	Matthew 11:28-30
Ezra is born, and we move to Cincinnati. Michael begins working as a youth pastor.	Outsider feelings. Not enough. I desire to appear perfect. Perfectionism and performance really plague me as a new pastor's wife.	My mission to want others to know God and make Him known.	Isaiah 48:10 Behold, I have refined you, but not as silver; I have tried you in the furnace of affliction.
Living in Cincinnati and identity.	I am faced with who I used to be.	2 Corinthians 5:17	Behold. I am making all things new.
We have four kids in four years and I am given way more than I can handle.	Control	I begin to feel free from the yoke of slavery of perfection.	Galatians 5:1 2 Corinthians 12:9-10
Michael's pastoral candidate process.	I am not enough. I am not ready.	I don't have to be enough, Christ's power is made perfect in weakness. I don't have to be ready, God will equip me.	Matthew 28
I finally spend time grieving the death of my mother and unraveling the lies from my past.	Control, perfection	Galatians 5:16-17 Refining faith is messy. I don't have to control all things. God is in control. He holds me up. He sustains me.	Ephesians 6
Now, I still am able to identify the lies that Satan uses to make me feel shame, fear, and doubt.	I am alone. I am not enough. I am not right. I am an outsider. I need to be stronger. I have to appear perfect. If I can control my world and what others see, I won't hurt again.	2 Timothy 2:22 So flee youthful passions and pursue righteousness, faith, love, and peace, along with those who call on the Lord from a pure heart.	Exodus 17:12 Who is holding up your hands? Who knows what makes you limp? Who helps refocus you to the truth of the gospel, Christ in you, the hope of glory.

224

Your Story:

Life Event	Lie you believed	Truth that sustained you	Scriptures to help you shed gospel light on this season

Chapter 12: Questions for Personal Reflection or Small Group Discussion

1. Read and mark Deuteronomy 6:5-7. Write about the things we are called to do in our relationship to the Lord. What are we supposed to pass on to our children (or those we influence)?

> *You shall love the Lord your God with all your heart and with all your soul and with all your might. And these words that I command you today shall be on your heart. You shall teach them diligently to your children and shall talk of them when you sit in your house, and when you walk by the way, and when you lie down, and when you rise* (Deut. 6:5-7).

2. How do your specific idols distort the things you pass on to your children or those you influence?

3. Read and mark 1 Samuel 16:7. What is the Lord concerned with when it comes to us and our children (or those we influence)? How is this different from the way our culture desires for us to raise our children or influence others?

> But the Lord said to Samuel, "Do not look on his appearance or on the height of his stature, because I have rejected him. For the Lord sees not as man sees: man looks on the outward appearance, but the Lord looks on the heart" (1 Sam. 16:7).

4. Read and mark John 14:27. How does the gospel free us from comparison? How can comparison keep us from peace?

> Peace I leave with you; my peace I give to you. Not as the world gives do I give to you. Let not your hearts be troubled, neither let them be afraid (John 14:27).

5. Read Ephesians 2:8-9. Rewrite the main idea of this verse in your own words. How can this verse be intentionally taught to our children (or those we influence) as we walk alongside them in the now and the not-yet?

> *For by grace you have been saved through faith. And this is not your own doing; it is the gift of God, not a result of works, so that no one may boast* (Eph. 2:8-9).

Chapter 13: Story Work

What are the voices you hear when you find yourself in a moment of loss, suffering, or pain? Is this voice redeemed or unredeemed? What are some scriptures that could help you gospel-waltz away from any unredeemed voices you may hear in moments of pain and suffering?

Chapter 13: Questions for Personal Reflection or Small Group Discussion

1. Read Ephesians 6:10-11. Why do we need to be intentional about relying on the Lord's mighty power?

> *Finally, be strong in the Lord and in the strength of his might. Put on the whole armor of God, that you may be able to stand against the schemes of the devil* (Eph. 6:10-11).

2. Name a time within the past year when you have needed to put on the full armor of God to fight against the devil's schemes. What did this look and sound like? How did you step out of the lies you believed?

3. Read Ephesians 5:13. Where is Satan's power thwarted? List all the properties of light and write about things we can do to bring our shame and the lies we believe into the light.

> *But when anything is exposed by the light, it becomes visible*
> (Eph. 5:13).

4. Read and mark Exodus 17:12. How is this an illustration for "alongside" community? Think about Moses' condition and list his personal flaws. Who comes alongside you to hold up your hands?

> *But Moses' hands grew weary, so they took a stone and put it under him, and he sat on it, while Aaron and Hur held up his hands, one on one side, and the other on the other side. So his hands were steady until the going down of the sun* (Ex. 17:12).

5. Read and mark Psalm 38:14, Matthew 5:4, Revelation 21:4, Proverbs 3:5, and Matthew 11:28-30. What examples does God give us for living in gospel-centered community?

God is near to the brokenhearted and saves the crushed in spirit (Ps. 34:18).

Blessed are those who mourn for they shall be comforted (Matt. 5:4).

He will wipe every tear from their eyes, and death shall be no more, neither shall there be mourning nor crying nor pain anymore, for the former things have passed away (Rev. 21:4).

Trust in the Lord with all your heart and do not lean on your own understanding (Prov. 3:5).

Come to me all who are weary and heavy-laden, and I will give you rest.... for I am gentle and humble in heart and you will find rest for your souls (Matt. 11:28-30 NASB).

Pick one of the verses you just marked and write about how God specifically cares for the broken. How is this care in gospel-centered culture different from our cultures in the world?

Chapter 14: Your Story

Walking forward in your redeemed, unraveled story, write how you will work towards shalom-peace as you gospel-waltz along with others in the now and the not-yet. How can your uniquely woven story impact those around you? Practice telling your story to others in your small group.

Chapter 14: Questions for Personal Reflection or Small Group Discussion

1. Read and mark Ephesians 6:13-18. List the elements of the armor of God and their purposes.

> *Therefore take up the whole armor of God, that you may be able to with-stand in the evil day, and having done all, to stand firm. Stand therefore, having fastened on the belt of truth, and having put on the breastplate of righteousness, and, as shoes for your feet, having put on the readi-ness given by the gospel of peace. In all circumstances take up the shield of faith, with which you can extinguish all the flaming darts of the evil one; and take the helmet of salvation, and the sword of the Spirit, which is the word of God, praying at all times in the Spirit, with all prayer and supplication. To that end, keep alert with all perseverance, making sup-plication for all the saints* (Eph. 6:13-18).

2. Using Ephesians 6:13-18, why does Paul close his letter to the Ephesians with instructions to put on armor? When do you need this armor?

3. Define shalom-peace.

4. Read John 14:27. How can we embrace shalom-peace when we feel suffering in the now and the not-yet of this life?

> *Peace I leave with you; my peace I give to you. Not as the world gives do I give to you. Let not your hearts be troubled, neither let them be afraid* (John 14:27).

5. How can shalom-peace transform us? How can shalom-peace transform the new society within the church?

Additional Extension for Story Work

You will need: construction paper, markers, glue, scissors, and a picture of yourself from the neck up.

1. Cut out and glue your picture from the neck up onto an 8.5x11 piece of construction paper.

2. Use markers to draw a body.

3. Fill in the body with the wounds, lies, and vows from your unique story.

4. On a separate sheet of construction paper, cut out a covering for yourself. God makes a covering for our shame with the righteousness of Christ. On this covering, write what God says is true about you in Jesus.

5. Then fold the covering like an accordion. Fold it back and forth like you would fold a fan.

6. Tape the covering just under your neck.

7. Lastly, one thing I talk about with the women in my small groups are the things that help us remember we are covered with the righteousness of Christ: gospel-waltzing in community with others. We remember our shame is paid for and covered when we are self-aware, aware of the truth in God's Word, and are praying for gospel-transformation in our hearts alongside others. So, surround the now-covered body with scriptures or prayers that remind you (and that you may memorize) to keep you gospel-waltzing and living as God has called you to live.

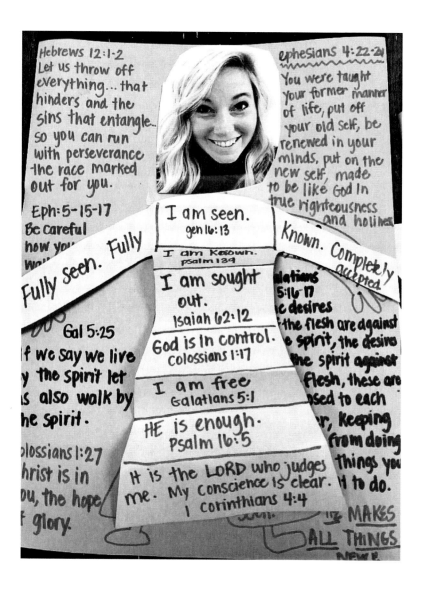

Notes:

Notes:

Notes: